HOLDING ON

*However hard we try
we can't hold on to time.*

ISBN 978-1-9993664-6-9

This edition published in 2022 by

THE LIME PRESS
1 LIME GROVE
RETFORD
DN22 7YH

HOLDING ON

ON

INSIDE THE HEAD OF AN OCTOGENARIAN

By
BARRIE PURNELL

ACKNOWLEDGEMENTS

Thanks to all of my friends. Life would be nothing without them.

CONTENTS

Page No.

CONTENTS (cont.)

Page No.

HOLDING ON TO EXPERIENCE (cont.)

HOLDING ON TO LIFE

HOLDING ON TO LOVE AND FRIENDSHIP

Love is greater than the wisest mind, and friendship is greater than love.

HOLDING ON
Until I learned the meaning of friendship I hadn't learned anything.

When everything was shutting down
And the sun stopped shining through,
When the gods started calling in
All my debts that had come due,
I turned in upon myself
From others I withdrew,
On my own, but not alone
While holding on to you.

It's easy to play on a sunshiny day
But where do you go when it rains,
And old friends leave you one by one
Until only their memory remains?
I could have succumbed to solitude
My remaining friends were few,
I found relief and kept belief
By holding on to you.

I knew you could keep secrets
That's why I told you mine,
And if you've read my poetry
You have looked inside my mind.
You know me so very well
I could tell you nothing new,
I kept my faith and felt safe
When holding on to you.

I hope future days are even better
Than those that we have shared,
My times have been made better
Just because you cared.
I crossed many frontiers
Searching for a better view,
But see no better place to be
Than holding on to you.

You know I am nearly there
You'll help me across the line,
Seems I've known you forever
Although it's really a shorter time.
They say you can't buy friendship
So it follows it must be true,
It is by chance or circumstance
That I'm holding on to you.

Friendship can be so close to love
That the join cannot be seen,
Friendships are like treasures
They are few and far between,
They define what's in our past
And what's in our futures too,
That's why I intend, until the end,
I will be holding on to you.

(To Lesley & Patricia July 2021

LOVE IN THE PRESENT TENSE
You can never love someone as much as you miss them.

In the night is when it hurts the most
When darkness is waiting to attack,
The mind playing silence on repeat,
Every shadow with a doubt attached.
I know endless grieving makes no sense,
Love only has meaning in the present tense.

Back when we laughed and cried together,
We never thought about tomorrow but it still came,
It never crossed our minds it wouldn't be forever,
We always thought that we could stay the same.
We were in love with no use for common sense,
Love only has meaning in the present tense.

I remember the autumn colours in her hair,
The taste of her kisses soaked in wine,
Memories now slowly fading into the past
Like an upended hourglass leaking time.
It's harder now to keep up the pretense,
Love only has meaning in the present tense.

I thought I'd captured her soul in my body,
I tried to paint a hole in the light of the day,
I felt the wind freeze my tears when I saw
The blood on the roses of our broken bouquet,
Then found it was just reality in suspense,
Love only has meaning in the present tense.

The clouds are forming faces in the sky,
They are just the silhouettes of my regret,
Evening holds onto the bones of the day
Skeletons of love are now all I can expect.
I live as a prisoner of love's past events,
Love only has meaning in the present tense.

I've reached another turning of the page,
Another unwanted churning of the day,
I feel I'm standing on the edge of truth
With the honesty of memory in decay.
I'm at the mercy of what the mind invents,
Love only has meaning in the present tense.

If only once again I could rest my head
In the welcome shelter of those soft brown eyes,
I'm blessed only by her ghost with open arms
And thoughts conceived between her thighs.
My soul ripped open by life with no defense,
Love only has meaning in the present tense.

Your first love is always perfect until you meet your second love.

First Love is a random collision
But somehow it lingers in the mind,
It takes such a long time to die,
It takes such a long time to find.

We were strangled and entangled
In a love that wouldn't go away,
Two lost souls in the same sad skin,
Searching for a better game to play.

The only things that she let me see
Were the parts I wanted to believe,
Her smile hid all the secrets
I was hoping to retrieve.

Hidden behind prurient promises
With her hair cut like Joan of Arc,
I knew I'd never breach her armour
Unless I could make it through her dark.

She held me sucked inside her kiss
Hiding me inside her eyes,
Then left me dancing with her shadow
In that desert where first love dies.

We had so much time and pain to kill
I was searching prophets for the truth,
While she was tearing off the petals
From the rose held in my mouth.

I saw her every time I closed my eyes.
I hummed the songs she used to sing.
Nothing's left of what was mine,
I took it all then lost everything.

We both broke all our promises,
We were damned right from the start,
Finding love without trust is nothing,
Like nails driven through the heart.

I still remember the taste of her lips
It doesn't matter what was gained or lost,
She is hardly even a memory now,
When it comes to love you don't count the cost.

You find your first love is a lesson
That love is something you cannot control,
And it is the cracks of that first heartbreak
That will let love leak back into your soul.

WAVING
Life is unfair and does not get better with time, you just get used to it.

I am waving to the lovers
About to leave each other's side,
Having given each other everything
They have nothing left to hide.
Although she holds her head up high
Her eyelids hang down low,
She didn't have the courage
To say she didn't want to go.

I am waving to the immigrants
Setting sail for shores unknown,
With a handful of false promises
And nowhere to call home.
Their ship sails on forever
On an ocean of their fears,
The image of our indifference
Reflecting in their tears.

I am waving to the virgins
Who, since love's tragedy began,
Have had their trust betrayed
By each and every man.
Where they looked for tenderness
They only found despair,
Their dreams and broken hearts
Lie scattered everywhere.

I am waving to the unborn child
And those who died before their time,
To the brides left at the alter
To all the victims of a crime,
Those deserving of our sympathy
But who never get enough,
Our self-pity all-consuming
With no room left for love.

I am waving to the soldier
Who laid down his life for me,
To the many tortured martyrs
Whose suffering made me free.
I hide behind my cowardice
With a message on a wreath,
Unsure if I would stand behind
The courage of my belief.

I am waving to those old friends
Who left and never did return,
Am I weeping for their loss
Or because soon it'll be my turn?
They melt into my history
And before their features fade,
I fix the image in my mind
Of the parts that they all played.

I am waving to my memories
That are trying to get lost,
Paid for with my suffering
I never added up their cost.
I know of everyone I loved
I loved her the best,
I will still be waving to her
When I've forgotten all the rest.

WASTED WORDS
There is no good way to waste words.

The list is long of the words that I have wasted
On truth and anger, trying to make some sense of love,
Tearing down my life stone, by stone, by stone,
Wishing I could start over. If only wanting was enough!
I am just another piece of broken art on display,
Just another perfect moment love threw away.

I am living through the summer of my discontent
My flowers wilt with the guilt of wasted time,
Surrounded by the changing shapes of a shadowed life
My feet stumble across the demons in my mind.
I thought I still had time but somehow I've misplaced it,
I thought I had the answer but time has now erased it.

When the clouds break above your best intentions,
And the numbing rain falls down on that last kiss,
And distance lays her heavy head beside you,
You hold the taste of that defeat upon your lips.
Lovers always know what torments you the most,
Hurt arrives unexpectedly, like death threats in the post.

I always thought that love was made of truth
But found that the memory often lies to the heart,
Hiding the answer to the lover's question
Just how and why do love's failures start?
Many promises are broken before you get love right,
Many hearts are broken by holding on too tight.

I'm tired of counting the odds just to make things even,
While the pawnshop kings hawk their souls for gold,
And the corner queens make promises of Eden
While knowing all their dreams are oversold.
I see my childhood hero's deeds are overturned,
Their medals unpinned and their honours returned.

My love was all adrift on my own private ocean,
I was on a course heading west past the sun,
With a crew of love's other losers I'd chosen,
The voyage damned before it had begun,
I tried to leave behind the guilt and the shame,
Knowing even if innocent the guilt would remain.

I collected all the thoughts of my remembered love,
And stored them in a box underneath my bed,
But there is nothing I can do that will ever erase
Those memories of love that I keep in my head.
My time for love is past now, I stand here alone,
Like a bird waiting for the wind to carry me home.

UNTIL ONLY KINDNESS REMAINS
Forever has not made loss forgettable, only bearable.

My world is getting old, starting to show a few rips
I am hanging on to the edge by my fingertips,
Today's virtue lost west to where the sun went to die,
It's so hard to see truth when you're part of the lie.

Holding on somewhere between memories and scars
With infinity whispering lost lines into my ears,
Slow motion falling away from what was once mine,
Seeing forever as just another moment in time.

Day and night merge slowly into a darker blue
The moon not sharp enough to cut its way through,
Thoughts arrive like terrorists hijacking my dreams
Taking me into darkness until dawn intervenes.

We grew up together our roots always entangled,
Pain inevitable when our contract was cancelled.
Her leaving did not mean I loved her any less,
I still had her letters but with no return address.

Her reflection's in the window where light is strong,
A suspicion of her voice in the silence of our song,
Technicolour dreams of yesterday memory unlocks,
Everything turning black when the music stops.

I throw a shroud over all of the words that I say
Muting the colours and making all meanings grey,
Memories once bright on the canvas of my mind,
Their colours now fading bleeding outside the line.

Rescued from an ocean of past blindfolded lovers
Whose unspoken treachery love always uncovers,
Just another pretender who's been caught in the net
Trying to ignore an absence that I cannot forget.

She was the last tragedy I so proudly painted,
The catalyst for me and sorrow to get reacquainted,
The canvas was torn letting the darkness back in,
I saw love was just the brighter side of suffering.

It's too long since she has seen my voice in ink
Only the echo of our song maintains the link.
In some quiet moment I may put that music on,
In those very moments it's like she's never been gone.

I am filling my life with empty memories of you
Until my version of amnesia starts to seep through.
Obsession and passion once ran hot through my veins,
Even their ghosts are now gone, only kindness remains.

WRITTEN DOWN IN BLUE
They discovered the distance that love couldn't cross.

I tried to write this with humour,
These lines I knew were overdue,
But in these times of heartbreak
Could only write it down in blue.

Beneath the sky far from the stars
They looked for answers, there were none,
They seemed to be just marking time
Chasing laps around the sun.

Caught unawares somewhere between
Being good friends and making love,
However long they talked online
They knew it was never quite enough.

They were trying to keep their distance
Within a space two meters wide,
They were running really low on love
Their hearts' left unoccupied.

Pretending they were face to face
When they were really miles apart,
Withdrawing one look at a time
Waiting for real life to restart.

Rooms all had too much space,
Caution and quarantine combined
To make them live like strangers,
Talking behind a hashtag sign.

No one can foretell the future,
You cannot forget the past is true,
There was nothing to be done but wait
Until the plague had passed on through.

I know they will look back with regret
At all of the chances that were missed,
I hope at least they will remember
The taste of the lips that they once kissed.

They never even scratched the surface
Of all the things they said they'd do,
Those times put the sad in all the lines
That I have written down in blue.

(In the aftermath of COVID 19 in 2021)

A FUNNY KIND OF LOVE
Sometimes a love affair can only be in the mind.

We were floating in a sea of self-deception
Our loyalties in conflict with the heart,
Doomed by the reality of mortality
Where living had become the hardest part,
And passion was a path we could not tread,
As we were lovers only inside our heads.

We walked arm in arm down coastal paths
Looking out to where the ships were sailing,
Our abandoned footprints dissolving in the sand
Along the line where the waves were breaking,
Our thoughts intertwined like spider's webs,
But we were lovers only inside our heads.

We strolled through narrow streets, past windows
Full of inept art and dubious treasures,
Knowing, without speaking, what we both thought,
Eyes carrying joy and sadness in equal measure,
Holding each other closer than we intended,
But we were lovers only inside our heads.

We travelled winding roads into wooded hills,
To eat light, healthy lunches in pleasant places,
Allowing us to continue a lover's pretence
Feeling safe In front of the unfamiliar faces,
Where word of our closeness wouldn't be spread,
Because we were lovers only inside our heads.

There was a limit to how much we could share,
No words could paint the pain upon her face.
Her smile was rainbow graffiti on a concrete wall,
Melting anger away and filling the space.
She knew I was feeling her hurt at what lay ahead,
Because we were really lovers inside our heads.

Our future now looked much shorter than our past
As she looked at me through the filter of her tears,
In a world slipping ever further from our grasp.
I held on to the moment to keep as a souvenir
Knowing our hearts were destined to be parted,
And that we were lovers only inside our heads.

We talked of God's addiction to suffering and pain,
Knew, if only we could see it, we'd understand infinity,
Wondered how we'd cope as life neared its end,
Agreed everything we did was in the context of eternity.
Disguising desire leaving our hearts unguarded,
We stayed lovers but only inside our heads.

She found there was a freedom in surrender,
At a time when even her pain was hurting,
Realising that, apart from love, nothing we own
Can be taken with us on our final parting.
She told me her signals had not been misread
Because we were lovers inside her head.

I was seeing her through the waves of farewell,
Ink bleeding through pages where once I wrote her name,
I leant into her whisper but still couldn't hear
If she was speaking words of love or blame,
I believed they were words of love she said
Because we had been lovers inside my head.

She was a dreamer who found her truth in trouble,
I used my pen to write her words, she was my muse,
Without her my creativity was leaving,
Her inspiration a precious thing to lose.
Now I'm lying in the dark of night in bed
With only fading images of her inside my head.

DISQUIET OF THE HEART
The best gift for your lover is honest friendship.

You who steal love wherever you find it,
Looking for the last shred of true love in the dark,
Finding love through theft
You know all that's left is
The disquiet of the heart.

Look past lust's immediate pleasure,
It's merely a shallow satisfaction leaving no mark,
Just a play you are staging
That's still not assuaging
The disquiet of the heart.

Don't give up your search until you find
A deeper love in which soul plays a greater part,
Love that lasts and is real,
Giving it time to heal
The disquiet of the heart.

You who demand proof before belief
Can't see the answer was with you from the start,
When your lover's your friend,
That's when you will end
The disquiet of your heart.

MUSIC
Music is one of the last links to my former self.

Music is the language of my memory, poetry
delivered straight to my heart, bringing me
one step closer to what used to be. It hijacks
my senses and defines my mood, I carry it's
rhythm inside me in my heartbeat, like love,
more felt than understood.

Songs paint pictures onto the empty silence
forming words from my feelings, phrases
falling like raindrops onto the still lake of
my emotions. The lyrics are like bookmarks
for the mind, tracking the history of my
elation and my heartbreaks.
.

Some music brings melancholy and pain
that drips out of me like blood. I crawl
into the space between the notes so I can
hide from my own thoughts, comforted by
a song that lets me know at least one other
person feels just as I do.

It is poetry that elevates music into a song, an
unconscious exercise in philosophy, as close
as I may get to a spiritual experience. For all
my inner indecisions, when self-doubt is all
I've got, the clairvoyant certainty of music
points the way to an escape.

I need music, and a lyric that rhymes, to see me through my dark and lonely times. When I'm sitting on the ashes of my life, face to face with all of my past regrets, I hear one of my favourite tracks leaking from a stranger's headphone backs, a song that was a page of my past life.

I was sad because it made me think of *her*.
I was glad *because* it made me think of her.

FLYING SOLO
Just take the risk, all life is an experiment.

All of us at some time will
Realise we're flying solo,
Into an unknown future
An always new tomorrow.
Time removed friends and lovers
Who gave me all I know,
My co-pilots of long ago
Who kept me flying.

Through the unpredictability
Of capricious circumstance
I found myself flying alone again,
A penalty of singular romance.
I'd forgotten the music
And the steps of the dance,
I'd have to take a chance
Or die trying.

If the voices in my head were mine
They told me things I didn't mean,
There were many things in my mind
I wish I hadn't seen,
Positivity being crowded out
By what might have been,
Not heaven or hell but in-between,
Heartaches inviting.

I listened to words that danced
On the lips of strangers,
Like gibberish spilling out
From the lips of angels,
As if their mouths alone
Could breathe an answer,
To why mortality's a stranger
When we know we're dying.

I concluded we are nothing
But what we have become,
We are spitting out our lies
But with an apologetic tongue.
I complained about my fate
Knowing nothing could be done,
Believing I was the only one
Left here crying.

I tried to make sense of my life,
To look behind my fear,
Broken hope left a gaping hole
In the faith I once held dear.
I wrote words that showed me stuck
Between guilty and sincere,
The way back to sanity not clear
Except by writing.

Pools of alphabetic failure spilled
Torpid verbs across my page,
Each one just a replica
Of one from a previous age,
When poets searched for
Another war to wage,
Another generation to engage,
With their proselytising.

These were just worthless words
That I was setting free,
From a guilty conscience
With an innocent plea,
Trying to re-attach with words
Broken feelings from my history
Into a comforting memory,
New start inviting.

I was being held down
By love and gravity,
Hoping that writing would break
The chain and set me free
From the heavy clouds
Of my misery,
And restore my buoyancy
So I'd be flying.

I'm flying solo now with just
A cobweb of apprehension,
Finding solitude the source
Of new-found inspiration,
Knowing, but not afraid of,
My final destination,
The ghosts of my imagination
Fuel my writing.

THEY ONLY ASKED ABOUT LOVE
For boys love is just a word used to manipulate girls.

They sat there in front of me in ordered rows
With fresh scrubbed faces and school uniform clothes.
They were waiting for a sort of history lesson
During which they could ask me any question,
About what my eighty years had taught me.

The boys wanted to know about my fast cars
And if I knew anything about any wars.
I spoke of my Bentley and Lotus Twin Cam,
And read lyrics of songs about the war in Vietnam.
The girls only asked me about love.

The boys asked if I had any advice I could give
About how to make money and how long to live?
I said if making money is easy I've not found it yet,
And you'll want to live longer the older you get.
The girls only asked me about love.

The boys asked if I'd like to go to Mars or the Moon,
And if we'd find aliens any time soon?
I said no to space flight I'd keep my feet on the ground,
As for aliens they may be already around.
The girls only asked me about love.

To girls who asked about love I said, men wiser than me
Have tried to define what love is and failed to agree,
It's something only you'll know, love's inside your brain,
A longing inside your heart your head can't explain,
But I know the girls already knew about love.

HOLDING ON TO HUMOUR

A sense of humour is the mind's immune system.

ICONS

My youth left me too quickly and it never came back.

I will never be an icon
Icons best die in their youth,
I have now lived far too long
So people know the truth.

Icons live their lives so fast
They have no time for regrets,
Driving Porsche550 Spyders
Or Flamingo Pink Corvettes.

Although heroes are remembered
Icons never really die,
Their deeds becoming greater
With every year that passes by.

James Dean was an icon
As was Marilyn Monroe,
Bob Dylan's one and he's alive,
Perhaps he doesn't know.

I could have been an icon
I was an unknown name,
But fortune never found me
And I never found the fame.

I had all the attributes,
Fast motorbikes and cars,
Handsome in an unlit room
Or to women drunk in bars.

I never made the breakthrough
Into films or the music scene,
So nobody will ever know
How good I might have been.

I suppose I should have taken drugs
And wrecked a hotel room,
But I was raised a Methodist
And born ten years too soon.

I might have married someone famous
But wasn't quite handsome enough,
In the end fate intervened
And I married her for love.

There are always all the poems
What I have gone and wrote,
Maybe at my funeral
They might dig out a quote.

So an icon I will never be
On that you can depend,
I've no more to say on icons
So I suppose that is the end.

THE PAIN OF FAME
Fame and good fortune are not often fellow travellers.

This is the story of Daniel Dune
Who boasted to pain he was immune.
At school he charged a penny fee
To let kids kick him in his knee,
And for an extra fee of two jam tarts
He'd let them kick his tender parts.
But Daniel's long suffering teacher
Thought he was a useless creature,
Whose only bits of learning came
Through the frequent use of cane.
He was often summoned to attend
Headmaster's study, and to bend
Into touch your toes position,
Where he smiled in quiet derision
As head with target well defined
Gave him six on his behind.
But Daniel felt no sensation
Adding to his reputation,
For being able to sustain
A high degree of personal pain,
Just a hint of what was to come
For the boy with the unfeeling bum.

He left with no certification
And very little expectation,
When into his lap did drop
A job in local butcher's shop.
All went well until the day
He was barged out of the way
By grumpy, fat, old, Mrs Spicer,
Who pushed him against the bacon slicer,
Which was spinning very quick,
And by chance was set to thick,
When in an instant one by one
It took three slices off Dan's bum.

He felt no pain, so didn't turn round,
'Til pants and trousers both fell down,
When he saw to his surprise
His bum was only half the size,
The rest on the counter in three slices
Already marked up with the prices.
Butcher dialled for ambulance
To deal with Daniel's circumstance,
Although not in pain, his lack of cheek
Meant he was bleeding on the meat.

At hospital Doc said stupid twits
Where are all his missing bits?
Fetch 'em quick while he's still strong
So I can sew his bits back on.
They went back to the butcher's store
Told him what they were looking for,
But oh what a calamity,
There's only two slices and not three.
Butcher said oh deary, dear
We must have sold one slice I fear,
And looking in his order book
Said it was sold to a Mrs Took,
And this must be your lucky day
She only lives two streets away.

So off they rushed to Took's abode,
To whom the third slice had been sold,
But Took said sorry you're too late
Pointing to Dad Took's empty plate,
I gave it to him for his tea
Which he enjoyed as you can see.
Thinking it was from a well-bred Friesian
Not from someone's nether region,
Dad said he wouldn't be complaining
'Cause it was tasty and sustaining.

Back to butchers medics flew
Asking butch what he could do,
Butcher said he'd cut a sliver
Off his biggest piece of liver,
Medics said you are a pal
And raced back to the hospital.
Doc said I shouldn't make a fuss
But I was expecting Gluteus Maximus,
I'm not sure even with my skill
I can do the same with a mixed grill.
Dan was still laid on his face
For pieces to be sewn in place,
Doc to overcome this crises
Sewed liver between the two bum slices.
That is how it came to pass
Dan possessed a Kebab style ass.

Dan forgot about the scars he carried
Until the day that he got married,
When wife said, Daniel how come
You've got three stripes across your bum?
Dan told her the story of his accident
And surgery he underwent,
Wife said I think you are unique
And went straight down to the boutique
To buy the smallest Speedos she could find,
So she could show off Dan's behind,
When they were dés-hab-ill-é,
On their Spanish holiday.
Sure enough Dan's striped posterior
Won prize for best rear in Iberia.

Dan then got a job within construction,
Where he was given some instruction
On how to avoid injury and failure
When using the pneumatic nailer.
For about an hour all went well
When they heard his workmate yell,
Oh my god I think Dan's dead
He's got a nail stuck through his head,
When round the corner Daniel turned
Looking really unconcerned.
But he didn't look too fine
He looked a bit like Frankenstein,
The nail in his head was quite a sight
Going in the left and out the right.
How the hell did you do that?
Said foreman taking off his hat.
Dan said, easy all I did was cough,
Dropped me gun and it went off,
Saying, come on, don't mess about
Get on and pull this nail out.

So they tied a rope of propylene
Between the nail and construction team,
To stop poor Daniel's head from moving
They jammed it between some railing tubing,
And with a countdown, one, two, three,
With one big pull the nail came free,
Together with a bit of Daniel's brain
Which he just kicked down nearest drain,
Saying, don't worry about that bit of grey,
I rarely used it anyway.
Come on now we must act real fast
Get me some Elastoplast,
And sticking a piece across each hole
Shinned back up the scaffold pole,

Where he immediately proceeded
To put more nails where they were needed.
When asked by boss if he would claim
Compensation for loss of brain,
All that Dan was heard to mutter
Was no, and at least it cured my stutter!

Later one day in November
The village assembled to remember
Guy Fawkes with a bonfire large,
And they put Daniel Dune in charge,
Because he was a celebrity
Due to his pain immunity.
So when the day eventually came
Dan set the big bonfire aflame,
He turned around tall and proud
To loud cheers from the watching crowd.
Then they started shouting, fire, fire,
In unison like a male voice choir,
Funny, thought Dan, I should know
I set it alight five minutes ago.
But crowd were getting more excited
Because Daniel was now backlighted,
By flames rising from his Burton's jacket
He was soon setting up an awful racket,
Dancing around like a man possessed
Trying to get himself undressed,
As those in the food van queue
Caught the scent of a barbeque,
Not realising that the smell did come
From fire reaching Dan's mixed grill bum.
So Dan's high degrees of Fahrenheit
At least enhanced crowd's appetite.

But Dan's fiery dance was to no avail
All his efforts were doomed to fail,
As from shiny shoes to smart coiffeur
Dan was burnt down to a cinder.
Sadly despite the efforts of his friends
This was how Daniel met his end,
And whatever else is said
Now that Daniel Dune is dead,
We see the fame we've been reviewing
In the end was his undoing.
It is a warning to us all,
Fame without life, is no life at all.

COME BACK CONCERT
Those idyllic teenage years were probably an illusion.

Just a sea of sad old singing faces
Trying to recapture their lost youth,
Immersed in sounds of yesterday
Trying to hide from the awful truth.

Swaying to the sounds of the ELO
The realisation of a longed for treat,
Trying their best to look so hip
But sadly clapping off the beat.

Tattoos that looked good at eighteen
Had lost their charm on wrinkled skin.
Tight branded T-shirts can't disguise
What a bad shape they're all now in.

Hyped up on a Costa Coffee fix
They dance to some imagined tune,
Their minds back in those far-off days
Of remembered teenage afternoons.

Inside the old heads of the fans
They're still all eighteen years young,
Their secret lives held safe inside
Until songs unlocking them are sung.

Cynicism hidden by the spotlight's glare.
The elders of rock bestride the stage
With thickening waists and thinning hair,
Trying to relive their glory days.

Only two of the original six survive
But fans care little about substitution,
It's the occasion they've come to savour,
Music to sustain their youth's illusion.

All good things must come to an end,
The elderly rockers shuffle off the stage,
The stadium empties, sad reality returns,
The not so youthful fans now feel their age.

At least their attempts to regain youth
Were carried out in company of their peers,
They had not embarrassed their progeny
And go home to resume their waning years.

It didn't take them very long
To resume their routine, boring lives,
Their dreams of reliving youth now gone
As they morph back into nine to five.

ON LINE DATE
Now dreams of love can be crushed in the privacy of your own home.

Life becomes more precious
When there's less of it to waste,
When opportunities for sin are few
And only slow girls can be chased.
So what is an old man to do
Except advertise their plight,
To seek a woman who says she will
Or even one who says she might?

I looked at all the dating sites
To find one where they were old,
But the personal advertisements
All appeared to be in code.
Eventually I found a site
That resolved my situation,
Inputting the unknown code
And receiving immediate translation.

I found that a BBW with GSOH
Was just a fat woman who laughed,
An MBL was married but looking,
And I needed to be photographed.
I had to add a truthful description
To join this so called agency,
Thinking right away that if I did
They wouldn't be queuing up for me.

But nothing ventured nothing gained
So I set about concocting,
A barely believable description
Of the persona I was adopting.
I found that GLWM, PR,
Was all that was required,
A good looking white male,
Professional but retired.

A ten year old photograph,
Taken in very dim light,
Was all that was necessary
To make me look alright.
With a touch of a button
My details were all set,
Available to all and sundry
On the internet.

I waited, my PC switched on,
With a degree of trepidation
To see if any woman would
Resolve my situation.
Within the hour upon my screen,
Against my expectation,
A dozen women had expressed
Interest in my information.

As I looked through the photographs
That looked out from the page,
I thought how young these women looked
Considering their age.
I thought it's probably because
They spend time in the gym,
And eat really healthily
To stay so neat and trim.

I picked out one I thought would meet
The criteria I'd specified,
And after on-line conversation
It came time to decide.
Should I take it further?
Should we agree to meet?
Should we just go for drinks
Or go somewhere to eat?

I thought a meal was safer as,
In case of stilted conversation,
Some good food and wine
Could well save the situation.
We arranged to meet
In an upmarket eatery,
To make a good impression
I said the bill would be on me.

I got there a bit early
And, in case of a mistake,
Looked around for exits
From which I could escape.
But there was only one door
As far as I could see,
So I'd be stuck with her
And she'd be stuck with me.

A woman entered on her own
Could she be the one?
And immediately I could see
She was no good at sums,
Because her picture and her age,
In the statement she had made,
Was very, very clearly
Out by more than a decade.

Although my description too
Flattered to deceive,
It was far too late now
For me to up and leave.
We exchanged names as we met
And shook each other's hands,
She said her name was Willamena,
And she told me she was Trans.

I thought well that explains
The beard and size twelve shoes,
And, from glimpses of her arm,
Those military tattoos.
Not wanting to be un-PC
I thought what could I do?
But just make the best of it
And see the evening through.

We had a drink and ordered,
Which she did with some delight,
I could see from her selection
She had a healthy appetite.
She said she started out as William,
A bricklayer by trade,
But changed it to Willamena
When she joined the Fire Brigade.

She said that tomorrow
When she came off shift,
If I agreed to meet again
She'd show me the fireman's lift.
I didn't like the direction
In which our talk was leading,
Any sort of Trans transaction
Something I wasn't needing.

I paid the bill, which said amount
I can say without a doubt,
Would have caused a poorer man
To take a mortgage out.
Conversation never faltered,
Which came as some relief,
But didn't change my intention
To keep our goodbyes brief.

I made some lame excuse
About getting back to my flat,
To let my old dog out
And feed a hungry cat.
I saw her to a taxi
And waved a quick goodbye,
Feeling a little guilty when
I saw a tear form in her eye.

So a lesson had been learned,
I had seen the light,
I would no more seek my solace
From an internet dating site.
It wasn't that she was overweight,
Or due to that, 'him to her', deceit,
I just could never fall for a woman
Who stood on size twelve feet.

LIMITATIONS
It's often too late when you find out your limitations.

Sarah had requested I go with her to the fair
That set up in the car park close up to the Square.
The fair had drawn the usual mixed and motley crowd
And every ride played music very, very loud.

Our first stop was the dodgems Sarah said, I'll drive,
Mum took her own car, I was strapped in at Sarah's side.
We started, and too late I realised Sarah's first decision
Was to achieve whenever possible a head on collision.

Parents with one arm around kids for protection,
Had to drive one handed so had poor direction,
Providing a tempting target for Sarah to enjoy
With her chosen policy of seek out and destroy.

She was driving with uncontrolled aggression,
I just closed my eyes until the ending of the session.
She then went on the centrifuge, with no fear at all,
Invisible forces holding her safe against the wall.

Sarah then approached the Waltzer, I tried to hide,
But was persuaded to climb the steps up into the ride.
As I approached I expressed some apprehension
The ride might not be suitable for someone on a pension.

I said to Sarah are you sure I'm not too old for this,
I really think I should give this one ride a miss?
I guarantee you'll be fine, was her quick repost,
It was only then I noticed she had her fingers crossed!

Sarah pushed me into the car, the safety bar slammed shut,
The mean looking controller retired into his hut.
He threw the electric switch and then released the brake,
I was already thinking this was a big mistake.

We started fairly gently the car was swinging round
Moving side to side, moving up and down,
But it was getting faster, I thought blooming heck!
My head was showing every sign of parting from my neck.

My stomach was also now starting to complain
Indeed every part of me was starting to feel the strain.
To make it worse young Sarah shouted to the man,
This is much too easy, so just give it all you can.

This caused the man with evil eyes to give us an extra spin
With total disregard of the old age pensioner within.
By now I was going a whiter shade of pale
My hands clutching desperately to the safety rail.

Then when death was imminent it began to slow,
I wasn't sure what was up and what was down below.
I was struggling bravely my stomach contents to retain
Vowing I'd never go a-waltzing with young Sarah again.

I had survived a journey with Sarah at my side
That for an octogenarian was near to suicide,
Back home this OAP reviewed the situation,
Concluding that, in fairground rides, I'd found my limitation.

(In 2021 with Sarah Bryn-Jones aged 11)

THE CONSIDERATE CAPTAIN
Vanity may be our most expensive sin.

We are all slaves to our own vanity,
Which was the cause of a calamity
Involving a ship and a woman's vanity
And her over-attachment to millinery.
This is the story of the good ship Bright,
Which put to sea on a stormy night,
With all her crew in excellent order
And twenty passengers safe aboard her.

Of ladies there were numbered ten,
And Captain gladly welcomed them,
As no matter what a sailor's grade is
He's always pleased to see the ladies.
Among them was the widow Pratt
Most notable for her distinctive hat,
She would never go out without it
Some say she's bald, and who would doubt it?

Her hat was certainly a sight,
Purple and green and very bright,
The captain, making conversation,
Complimented her on its colouration.
But as they sailed away they got a shock
When the ship hit a sunken rock,
Before the captain could express annoyance, he
Perceived his ship was losing buoyancy.

Passengers screamed, as they would do,
When they observed that all the crew,
Were removing lifeboats locking shackle,
Lowering them down on the bowsing tackle.
Hold back, said captain not so fast
Passengers first, the crew go last,
Adding just take your lead from me, men
And do your duty as merchant seamen.

We're going down lads but can do no less
Than give the ladies time to dress,
So my lads let's take it steady
All hands to the pumps until they're ready.
So the lads set to with a yo-ho-ho,
And pumped as fast as they could go,
Captain knew it wouldn't be long before
His motley crew would all be done for.

But within five minutes or even less,
Arrayed in various states of dress,
With many a curse and course remark
Passengers were ready to disembark.
All save one and that was widow Pratt,
The one with the outrageous hat,
Captain said, this wait's exasperating
Get down to her cabin, tell her we're waiting.

Sailor knocked on her door, and from inside
In a despairing voice widow Pratt replied,
I've lost my hat and regret extremely
To appear without it would be unseemly.
Captain said I know that our Mrs Pratt
Has never ever been seen without her hat,
So all hands stop pumping and look around,
The widow Pratt's hat must be found.

They gave the whole vessel an examination
Nothing escaped the crew's observation,
And by now the captain surely was thinking
I've got to do something my vessel's sinking.
The captain knocked on the cabin door
Saying, please come out madam I implore,
If it's about the hat I will promise you
We'll look the other way is what we'll do.

Captain said the water's rising by degrees
It's already risen way up past my knees.
Alright, if you promise, I'll delay no more,
Said Pratt, as she opened up the door.
Then Captain's curses could be heard,
As he uttered many profane words,
His hands shook and his face turned red
As he said, what is that upon your head?

Oh dear, said Pratt without a care,
I never thought of looking there,
By now water was up to her waist
And to the deck they both made haste.
But the water rose faster and faster
It was a maritime disaster,
They saved a hat but at what a cost?
The ship and all her hands were lost.

Soon nothing on the surface could be seen
Except one hat in purple and green,
Oh what a tale that hat could tell
As it bobbed up and down on the ocean swell.
They say if you're sailing around there at night
You may see a spectral ship by the name of Bright,
Drifting silently along the coast,
Crewed by a captain and a bald-headed ghost.

THE TALE OF CLARENCE CRUNCH
In Yorkshire authority is the enemy, tax is theft.

This is the tale of Clarence Crunch
Who led a very rag-tag bunch
That every day would sally forth
From a scrapyard up in t'north,
Hoping by happy circumstance
That he'd meet people who by chance
Had some objects for disposal,
So he could make them a proposal
To take their rubbish off their hands
While saying, they must understand,
That items of which they wanted rid
Were only ever worth a quid,
But as a friend he'd do his bit
'Though there was no profit in it.

So smiling, with his toothless gash,
He would offer them some cash,
When the oft delighted sellers
Would pass to him their family treasures,
Not realising in Clarence's system
They were just another victim,
His heart lost in the Yorkshire fog
He was meaner than his scrapyard dog.

Before long this old man's fortune,
Garnered by trading and extortion,
Grew fast because he was very lax
When it came to paying tax.
Then one day a tax inspector
Skilled in the recycling sector,
Forced poor Clarence to disclose
Why living was so grandiose,
When tax returns, signed off by bosses,
Showed company always making losses.

As the bank account was overdrawn
Inspector asked 'where's money gone?'
Clarence said it was obvious
Why his company made a loss,
He explained in his defense
It was due to size of the expense,
Required to keep his staff content
Withdrawal of labour to prevent.

Unbelieving tax inspector,
Pulling out his lie detector,
Asked why company car choices
Comprised nothing but Rolls Royces,
And wasn't it a bit outrageous
To have Christmas Party in Las Vegas?
Adding he thought that it was cheatin'
By claiming cost of kids at Eton,
On your forms you are maintaining
It's just a part of your staff training.
As for swimming pool, it's no solution
To claim it's part of staff ablutions.
No, there is no doubt Mr Crush
You're trying to make fools of us.

Clarence replied, now don't be rash
Before you take my hard earned cash,
I am sure we can make a deal
To your greed I will appeal,
What about a fat brown envelope
Or a holiday, I'm sure there's scope
For us two too agree
To forget my tax anomaly.

But inspector was a Baptist
What they preached so he practiced.
Mr Crunch, inspector said,
My morals you surely have misread,
You'll be charged by the judiciary
With tax evasion and bribery.

So it was Clarence was brought
To stand up in the county court,
Where he pleaded he was not guilty.
It was all due to his inability
To read the forms that he was sent,
As his youth had been misspent
Collecting rags to pay his rent,
And sifting coal tips to get fuel
Instead of going off to school.

As Clarence sat down on his rear
Both Judge and lawyer shed a tear.
Judge called lawyer forward on his own
And after conversing in hushed tone,
Judge said, Crush I sympathise
With what has led to your demise.
We find you in this situation
Because of lack of education,
So I've been as lenient as I can
And have agreed with your tax man
Half a million will clear your debt
Rest of it he will forget.
Clarence thought this deal
Just allowed tax man to steal
Half a million which by rights
Should still be in his safe at night,
But in his heart knew he'd been caught
So shook their hands and left the court.

No lessons learnt and unrepentant,
Just thinking he needed new accountant,
Clarence returned to his scrap
To make more money out of crap,
And over time became real smart
Raising tax evasion to an art.
So when at a ripe old age he died
His relatives could say with pride,
He may have only dealt in trash
But he made a load of cash,
Turning his profits into gold
So by the time that he was old
He had gold stashed everywhere,
In the attic, under the stair,
Of which taxman was unaware
As all the gold was undeclared.
All his relatives will say
Is they're still mining his gold today.

ODE TO IDLE
Graduation is not always a gateway to understanding.

This is the story of a man called Idle
The thought of work made him suicidal,
A tale of a man with a misspent youth
Who hated work and that's the truth.
At school he didn't give a damn
Cheating his way through his exams,
He only measured his success
By his degree of idleness.
At university he chose a subject
Where any answer could be correct,
Rejecting maths and technology
He chose some little known ology.
A thousand theories with no outcome
Just some bullshit wrapped in bunkum.
This is the course for me he said
Then I can spend more time in bed,
Study will be of no concern
As there are no facts to learn.
For my final dissertation
All I'll need is imagination,
To come up with a theory that will show
There are some things we'll never know.
Then with the rest of his idle squad
Idle with mortarboard was shod,
Graduating with a pass degree
In his chosen ology.

As parent's funding was now ceasing
Idle saw his debt increasing,
And he, God forbid, might have to work
Which didn't appeal to this idle Turk,
He wouldn't consider it success
To give up his life of idleness.

To alleviate his fiscal circumstance
He thought he'd give the dole a chance,
He was sure cash would be enough
To prevent him from sleeping rough.
So Idle signed on and took the cash
And, as long as he wasn't rash,
Found he could live an average life
Cause he had no children or a wife.
Idle's only problem lay
In what he was going to do all day,
Turning down the Gym and petty crime
He thought protesting could fill his time.

Climate change, anti-capitalism,
Anti-fracking or anti-fascism.
Anti-war, anti-migrant,
Anti-nuclear disarmament.

Anti-gender discrimination,
Pro-life or pro-immigration.
Women's rights, anti-abortion,
Anti anyone with a fortune.

Anti-stop and search, anti vax,
Anti-austerity and bedroom tax.
Black lives matter, anti-Brexit,
Anti-Israel and pro-Tibet.

Anti-royalty, pro revolution,
Anti a democratic constitution.
Anti-government and opposition,
Anti the use of the preposition.

What to choose was the only question
Where to make his intervention,
Any cause would find some room
Inside Idle's moral vacuum.
There was a local parish protest
With which he sort of acquiesced,
The one against the new by-pass
Which involved just sitting on your ass,
To stop the work that someone planned
On some rich bastard's private land.
That's for me, said our idle sod,
A chance to confront the local plod
Who he saw as being in possession
Of all the instruments of oppression.
So he offered up his services
For by-pass protesting purposes.
He waited patiently for his instruction
On how to obstruct by-pass construction.

They told him that his job would be
To stop the felling of a single tree.
So up into the tree he climbed
Leaving the ground way behind,
Onto the branches he held tight
And settled down to spend the night.
Before long he began to think
He may have had too much to drink,
Because he knew in actuality
He'd exceeded his bladder capacity.
Having realised this far too late
He had an urgent need to urinate,
Deciding in these circumstances
Those below would have to take their chances.

He couldn't hold on, so started to pee
From his perch up in the tree,
But his stream was intercepted
By a hazard he'd not detected,
In the form of a high voltage wire,
Which laws of physics did conspire,
To transmit back up poor Idle's pee
A large shock of electricity.
With a cry Idle and tree were parted
He landed back from where he started.
His fall was broken to his surprise
By a woman protester of ample size,
Who, at sight of Idle's tumescent member,
Thinking he might well attack her,
Jumped up to dislodge him from her tum
Increasing his upward mo-men-tum,
Bouncing him off past the assembled crew
Straight onto the barbecue,
And as if to complete the farce
He ran off with flames coming out his arse.

Idle's resulting loud cry of pain
Had alerted cops searching the terrain
For protesters secret location,
Their batons ready for a confrontation.
Somewhere a man was screaming,
And ever higher notes was reaching,
They saw why screams were getting higher
When they saw his backside was on fire.
Using their batons and CS gas
They soon extinguished poor man's ass,
And frogmarched his smoking remains
Back to the camp from whence he came.
Idle got no sympathy from his crew
Who blamed him for wrecking their barbecue.

Very soon this revolting band
Were locked up in a dark blue van,
And all of them feeling suicidal
Were in court awaiting law's reprisal.
They were fined fifty pounds a piece
And bound over to keep the peace.
Magistrate told Idle he was in the frame
To shoulder some additional blame,
And his fine would be fifty higher
For running around with an unguarded fire.

As Idle the court departed
He wished that he had never started
His protest career, which had ended
More quickly than he had intended.
And still he was intent to shirk
Anything resembling work,
But wanting to help his fellow man
On the campus he would stand,
Warning all remaining students
Not to join any protest movements.
A sorry sight to tell the truth
A warning to all the passing youth,
Of just how useless a man can be
Even with an ology degree.

HOLDING ON TO EXPERIENCE

*No one has it all figured out,
especially not the people who
are acting like they do and
judging you because of it.
Some things can only be
learned by surviving
your own journey.*

NORTH ROAD
I know however far I run my past will always be right there with me.

Between the red brick houses,
Where the parallel pavements rule,
Cars are decorated with fallen leaves,
Blue-blazered children are off to school.
House names half-hidden, origins lost
In forgotten memories, but history remains.
A million feet have polished the paths
In gardens washed clean by the rain.

I rest in the shadow of the sycamores
Remembering when love was freedom,
Nostalgic for a life I never really lived
Knowing there's no way back to Eden.
I'm walking alone with my memories
While my memories walk alone with me,
Realising we are all leading actors
In our own real-life tragedy.

People are on their way to church,
They will be today's congregation,
I now believe, where I once doubted,
I too am looking for salvation.
How lucky are those whose god
Will forgive their every sin,
And know that right and justice
Are always going to win.

The people passing feign normality
But have their reality defined,
By the fences of hypocrisy
Put up around their minds.
Each footstep another heartbeat,
A new doubt in every breath,
Will they ever amount to anything
But the ashes of their faith?

A Magpie in the high pine tree
Reflects the sorrow in lover's eyes,
Having overheard the confessions
Of hearts stripped of their disguise.
They've found that they are bound
By promises and all those things
They've become, and can't undo.
In the quiet, a lone blackbird sings.

Sun sets on the never dark streets
Only the echoes of love remain.
The road is paved with empty words
That have been written to explain,
Why we are all held prisoners
To everything our parents held dear,
Arguments between present and past,
Hostages to long remembered fears.

I head towards the shaded shadows
Time and distance vanish there,
Between the lines of hope and fear
Without the energy to care.
There is nothing left to salvage,
There is no one left to blame,
Most of those who pass me by
Will never even know my name.

If only I could read my mind
I'd see the truth of what used to be,
Before I sink below that place
That I once called memory.
Although life is going faster
I've done my best to make it last,
But it often seems my future
All lies within my past.

(*Walking down North Road in Retford, 2021*)

NEW EYES
A child sees the world differently as they are looking upward.

It's a wonderful day, one I've never seen before.
Trees reflect back from the canal's still waters,
Refraction in the surface reinforces their beauty.
Horses move like dancers in the adjoining pasture.

A surprising sunset breaks through the clouds,
I'd like to wrap my arms around this scene and save it,
Javelin like shadows chase across the fields,
If only I could take this picture home I'd frame it.

I'm with a child who looks at the world through new eyes
Without a thought about her own mortality,
Before long she will confront the frailties of maturity
Looking out through experienced eyes at reality.

We fought with words as weapons at twenty paces,
I couldn't hide when she had turned me inside out,
I was falling into a man who I didn't recognise,
I let her take me by the hand and pull me out.

I'll more often suspend reality to see the world
As this child sees it, instead of living blind.
If I listen to her wisdom and look into her world,
I may see everything with my horizons redefined.

I have spent a long time chasing after riches
When they were there around me all of the time,
I've been envying other men's possessions
Instead of looking at what was already mine.

I found contentment begins when comparison ends,
Our biggest trials are life lessons in disguise,
All the mistakes we make are to be learnt from,
We don't have to wait until we're old to be wise.

Now when I think of beauty it is the people
I love, or have loved, who come first to my mind,
I should have treasured them more dearly.
People you can love and trust are hard to find.

I now see beauty in people just for what they are
Those who have known defeat, suffering, and loss,
Their wounds and scars just evidence of a life lived.
I'm no longer taken in by beauty's surface gloss.

Oh to see the world again with a child's eyes
With our wonder able to overcome our fear,
Remembering that life is just a state of mind
With each new experience a precious souvenir.

I have seen myself becoming a servant of sadness,
A purveyor of melancholy and sorrow,
This is a waste of perfectly good happiness,
I resolve to live with optimism from tomorrow.

MERELY PLAYERS
We pretend to be who we want people to think we are.

You say everyone you meet's an actor,
Who tells you they are through with acting
And are ready to start another chapter.
Their denials are betrayed by the lies in their eyes,
You know people like this, showing you just the face
That they think you're after,
Hiding their real selves behind a mask of laughter.

In the play of life you are just one partner,
Knowing perception's what will decide
Who is to be the servant or the master.
Smiles on the lips hide words that don't escape
Which puts everything in doubt, like promises made
Where honesty's a factor,
By your closest friends or any other actor.

You see the evidence of their phony power
From behind their masks, and leaking from
The cracks in their masquerade tower.
They use you as a scapegoat for their own beliefs
Knowing they will leave, taking everything but your faith,
Another bankrupt defector,
Another broken soul searching for their honour.

Everyone you meet you'll find is just an actor,
Living a fake reality in costumes of deceit,
Spending their lives trying to fool each other,
Not bothering with truth when it's so easy to create it.
How can you even believe the promises of a lover,
Or the forgiveness promised by your Saviour,
When they may turn out to be just another actor?

SMALL MINDED MEN
The wisdom of modern man is only exceeded by his stupidity.

The world is full of small minded men
Drifting on waves of unawareness,
Suffocated by feelings of unfairness,
Navigating by the compass of their friends.

The world is full of small hearted men
Never feeling the grand affair's passion,
Or the ordinary heartbreak's satisfaction,
Untouched by the poet's insightful pen.

The world is full of small thinking men
Seeing the world from a singular position,
Paralysed by doubt and indecision
When confronted by more than one event.

The world is full of small souled men
Waiting for their god, like the prophet said,
To exorcise the devils in their head,
Dying many times before their last amen.

The world is full of small spirited men
Unconcerned by all of life's mystery,
Or by the lessons of their own history,
Living their lives only in the present tense.

The world is full of small minded men
Living only within their own horizon,
Unencumbered by the gift of vision,
Content to live their yesterday's again.

BEING DIFFERENT
There's no cure for being human, we can only embrace difference.

She's sitting alone in the chair
Nothing to hear but her breathing,
She covers her eyes with her hair
You can't see the fear that she's fighting.

She has run a long way from afraid,
She hides in the dark from confusion,
When you think that she has been brave
That is just another illusion.

Seeking out any chance for rejection,
A child hiding inside grown-up skin,
Bewildered by life's contradictions,
Trying hard to find some way to fit in.

She's so tired of doubting Thomases
And the lies that they all speak,
Their words wrapped up in promises
That no one seems able to keep.

She's run out of safe corners to hide in,
She is afraid of what she might be,
Too anxious for real life to begin,
Too afraid of what others might see.

She is hiding inside her own story
It's the safest place she'll ever find,
Only if her heart was inside me
Could I know what is inside her mind.

72

I tell her, don't apologise for existing,
Don't apologise for just being you,
Start accepting instead of resisting,
Don't paint your self-portrait in blue.

Don't run away from your imagination,
Find out what it means to be you,
Stop hiding behind fake distractions
Only you can determine what's true.

Some things you hear they're for leaving,
Hold on to those you know are for real,
They are the things worth believing,
But love is something you just have to feel.

Live life as if your dreams are all true,
Let love catch you anytime that you fall,
Remember the beautiful one's really you,
You're the one, in the end, who'll have it all.

(Being autistic can be like living in constant chaos.)

TWENTY FOUR HOURS
The young look to the future, the old try to recapture the past.

I'm in that alternate reality regime,
The space between waking and a dream,
Where I find that mix of hope and despair
We all carry inside, ready to emerge
And catch us unaware.

I wake leaving disquieting dreams behind,
Morning sun machineguns through the blinds,
In the house where everything knew my name.
I had returned home to find
None of the past remained.

Alone with only my phone and pills,
And a bundle of unmade plans with time to kill,
I'm here in the hollow of my heart
And the empty of my house,
Where the shadows of memory start.

I can't trust memories anymore
They're not the friends I knew before,
I want to go back to before my mind was black,
But life's not like a movie, you can't
Walk out and get your money back.

I look for recognition in the village street
But see indifference in the faces I meet.
The day passes in waves of strangers,
With just a spindrift of friends,
My attempt to resurrect the past a failure.

I returned to find the happiness of youth
But only found the bitter taste of truth,
That you cannot leave and yet still belong.
I must let go of the rose-tinted past,
I've been watering dead flowers for too long.

74

Vapour trails bleed across the sky
Catching the day's last slow goodbye,
The silver circled moonlight
Crests the waves of shadowed shapes
That walk with me into the night.

I feel myself falling into sleep,
As if my soul's trying to break free
But cannot quite uncombine.
I feel my body's present
But I cannot find my mind.

Images melt away like Dali's clocks,
As dreaming starts and reality stops,
The hurt of twenty-four hours ceased
With an irresistible drift into that safe place
Of deep sleep's inner peace.

A JOURNEY THROUGH TWO CENTURIES OF DEATH
I see life as a brief shaft of light between two eternities of darkness.

Stone pillars mark the entrance
To a graveyard of Victorian times,
A great copper beech stands
As this burial ground's concierge,
Unmoved by heavy limbed mourners
Passing in their sad cortege,
Or furtive lovers seeking solace
Under the cherries and the limes.

Golden needles clothe the path
Below a cathedral arch of pines,
A hundred years of history
Hidden by their time-chiseled bark.
Against their majesty mere humans
Struggle to make their mark,
We proceed quietly, as penitent pilgrims
Would approach a shrine.

An iron bridge connects the ancient
To those newly entombed,
Temporal limestone replaced
By marble more easily read.
A boy laughs, chasing his sister
Through this city of the dead,
Indifferent to the skeletons below
Who know he too is doomed.

I move reverentially between the
Serried ranks of marble and stone,
Engraved to record the birth and death
Of each exemplary life.
No liars or cheats are buried here,
No husband who beat his wife,
Where the evil men of this town lie
Will forever remain unknown.

Our journey is watched over
By a stone angel with a broken wing,
Inscriptions remind us of
Wars and plagues come and gone.
As if to defy death, gaudy artificial flowers
Sprout from the stone,
The grief of their custodians
Not deep enough for frequent visiting.

These monuments are not erected
For the dead but the left behind,
A reminder of their own mortality
And things they didn't say.
Prince, pauper and priest all find
Death is their common enemy,
Only by the ashes scattered
In their wake are they defined.

I stand facing the church,
Two centuries of death having been crossed.
Death once encountered cannot be unlearned,
It is the ultimate thief,
We survive life by subterfuge
Floating on an ocean of disbelief,
None know on which side of the grave
We will have to pay the cost.

Night's shroud brings other actors
To this amphitheater of sorrow.
A vagrant makes a bench his bed,
Every day for him a battle,
He knows among so many ghosts
His own spirit matters little,
Guarded only by the moon
He will dream himself into tomorrow.

Tomorrow I'll walk again beneath the pines
And smell the freshly mown grass,
The beauty of this Eden wasted
On all those held close by stone.
For some this is the only plot of land
That they will ever own,
I can but respect the memories they've left
And whisper thankyou as I pass.

(A walk through Retford cemetery 2020)

ROAD TO PARADISE
Only one problem with paradise, you've got to be dead to get in.

The preacher shouts his message
To the nearly empty pews,
With only a few bored choirboys
There to hear his news.
The congregation has gone missing
Because they have got wise,
They know he just wants a ticket
To his own pure paradise.

The politician tries to tell us
That he's doing his very best,
Everyone knows he's impotent
Just like all the rest.
He tells us it would be better
If we all took his advice,
But he just wants us to vote him
Into a seat in paradise.

The King sits on his throne
Trying as best he can
To persuade all of his subjects
He's really just like them.
But he knows in his heart
However hard he tries,
That everyone suspects his place
Is guaranteed in paradise.

The Pope sits in splendour
In the Vatican in Rome,
Calling on all Christians
To let God into their home,
But few bother to listen
To the Pontiff's forlorn cries,
They reject his plea to renounce all sin
Before they can enter paradise.

The millionaire sits in his mansion
With his young trophy wife,
And all the status symbols
Purchased in his life,
But his riches count for nothing,
You see sadness in his eyes,
As he realises that he can't buy
His way into paradise.

The general in his war room
Discusses tactics he will try,
Wondering how many casualties
He's able to justify.
His war is just, it must be won,
Lives must be sacrificed,
That's the price of peace
A hero pays to enter paradise.

The common man is not concerned
With a paradise to come,
His future is determined
By where he has come from.
He is not concerned today
About how or when he dies,
He's simply not expecting
To ever enter paradise.

I am wandering in confusion
While trying to recognise,
If the preacher or the vagrant
Is the true prophet in disguise.
Until I can find myself a god
Who is prepared to compromise,
I'll be left here searching for
My own road to paradise.

REALITY   (*Dementia Imagined*)
We are nothing more than an accumulation of our memories.

I need you to tell me the reason why
Things no longer appear the same,
Who has robbed me of reality?
I need to find someone to blame.

How do I know whose truth is true
Or if your truth is better than mine?
How do I know how far I have to go,
Or if I'll be able to get there in time?

I want to know how to tell if it's real
I have to know if it's really there,
I need to reach out my hand and touch it,
Know it's not just an illusion in the air.

I have mislaid the keys to pleasure,
I'm excluded from all of your games,
I don't want to go to your parties
Because I can't remember your names.

Can't make out the time that clock tells me
I know it's morning because now it's light,
I've a man in a box speaking the time
But how can I be sure that he's right?

Tell me how do I go about walking?
Are you sure that these legs are mine?
I know it wasn't all that long ago
These same legs were walking just fine.

I'd like to go out but I'm not certain
I would be able to find my way back,
I think you'd need to fit me with Satnav
To be sure I was on the right track.

Could I be in someone else's dream,
Is that why I seem to have lost control?
Or am I just some random neurons
Lost in the maze of an alien soul.

Why do you give me these tablets?
I think you are going too far,
You know that I cannot swallow
And I'm not even sure who you are!

Too many thoughts going through my head
I can't get them to slow down or stop,
My future is flowing away too quickly
I tried catching my past but let it drop.

I can't remember how things used to be
But for sure they were better than this,
Must be a reason for what's happening
Don't know what, but just know it exists.

Each night I dream that when I wake up
My world will be back to normal again,
Every morning I awake disappointed
With the same old disorganised brain.

I need something real to hold on to
Somebody close, and you are the one,
I need to hear your voice calling me back
Before it's too late and I'm already gone.

If I could find out who was responsible,
If I could only find who was to blame,
I'd ask them to tell me why they did it
If I could only remember my name.

TODAY
I think I could find the answer, if I could only find the question.

I do not understand the world I'm now in
Where it seems every her wants to be a him,
Where no one is happy in their own skin,
All wanting to inhabit the body of their dreams,
Aspiring to images seen on TV screens
Only achieved using artificial means.

People watching people, watching people on TV,
Why this is entertainment is just a mystery,
It seems anyone can now be a celebrity.
People's first meetings now far from discreet,
Getting naked just to find someone to meet,
We used to make do with just a face and feet.

The doctor writes prescriptions on his pad
For all those ailments we didn't know we had,
Giving out pills to cure you of happy and of sad.
Everyone's an expert on every medical threat,
Diagnosing any illness they haven't got yet
From symptoms looked up on the internet.

Influencers, the prophets of people's corruption,
Preach everyone must increase their consumption
Feeding the god of consumer compulsion.
They buy many items, real and imitation,
From far off factories, ignoring exploitation
Of workers involved in their goods preparation.

Images of the perfect life on social media sites
Encourage folk to expect more than is their right,
When they find that Nirvana remains out of sight
Ambitions are thwarted and all hopes are dashed.
Some seek their salvation at the bottom of a glass,
Others escape back into the comfort of their class.

They make declarations about love and wealth and sex,
Without any thought about what will happen next
Conversing with each other in emoji-littered text.
Morality and responsibility is replaced by indifference,
Relationships are short to the point of insignificance,
Contracts entered into with no thought of the consequence.

The world is warming, experts all say the same,
And if we are to believe them we are to blame,
So we have to wear sackcloth and admit our shame,
Admit we're the source from which all faults stem,
While pretend eco warriors are eager to condemn
Others who in truth are exactly like them.

Everyone's looking back to where their history begins
We are told we're responsible for our ancestor's sins,
It seems everyone's a loser and nobody wins.
To be proud of your country can now be a crime,
No account taken of attitudes changing with time,
I say you keep your history and I will keep mine.

Today we go to war with only our wealth to defend,
The enemy amongst us masquerading as our friend,
Those who speak the truth universally condemned.
Many banners are flying with reports flooding in
Of riots of confusion between the women and the men,
And fights between philosophers about morality and sin.
.

Yes the new world is a mystery to old folk like me,
Where you cannot believe what you hear or you see,
And everyone's intent on rewriting their history.
How could we have known before the internet arrived,
And we were playing those stacks of old forty-five's,
That those would be the best days of our lives?

HOMELESS
If you want to be invisible, try being homeless on the street.

I passed her half-hidden in the doorway
Only her eyes spoke of her pain,
Her history could not be imagined by me
Who had lived a life of constant gain.

What journey led her to this destination?
What escape routes were rejected on the way?
What fears drove her from home's security?
What caused her to throw her youth away?

I should have offered help and comfort to her
But she looked out with cold-eyed suspicion,
But what comfort could I offer? Only money,
Not the love needed to remedy her condition.

I was living a life of indulgent satisfaction
She was living one of unsatisfied need,
The love I should have given freely to her
Proved to be a love tarnished by my greed.

I looked away, I couldn't hold her gaze,
Trying to leave my guilt with her in the doorway,
Hoping to forget the injustice of my action
And the words I wanted to, but did not, say.

My history cannot be re-written,
My cowardice an arrow drawn in time,
Which is pointing at me standing here,
With that haunting picture burned into my mind.

I will think of her whenever I pass that street
And wonder if she ever made it through,
Knowing that but for the vagaries of fate
That lost soul could have been me ..... or you.

EMBRACE
I am not the mistakes that I made before.

It is a cold, blue sky winter's day,
I have empty pages and a frozen pen,
Ideas like the diamond frost melt away,
I'm locked up in myself again.
I did make some poor choices
Becoming lost in the contraflow,
Seduced by darker voices
A thousand embraces ago.

My head was telling me something
That my eyes just could not see,
Mistakes made in my choice of king
And the man I wanted to be.
Wrapped up in my coat of words
Never letting the real self show,
Looking for love I couldn't afford
A thousand embraces ago.

I left my prayers with my old God
There were pleasures I couldn't resist,
My mind fixed on love's frequent frauds
And many things that don't exist.
All the promises I could not keep,
All the truths only dead men know,
All the Judas kisses drowned in sleep
A thousand embraces ago.

The black clad priest addressed me,
With a subtle condescension,
The mysteries he tried to make me see
Were beyond my comprehension.
I saw no easy path to righteousness
There was too much pride to swallow,
Too many sins in which I'd acquiesced
A thousand embraces ago.

I was sitting where the stained glass
Let the evening sunlight filter in,
Hoping the words of the sacred mass
Would serve to cancel out my sin.
I joined in the hallelujah chorus,
I made sure to sing it slow,
Like I heard Leonard do before me
A thousand embraces ago.

Take this as my last confession
As I have nothing left to say,
This will be my final genuflection
For all those missed previously.
For all the love that I misplaced
With nothing left to show,
For all the lovers left in haste
A thousand embraces ago.

FORGETTING
Will I be remembered for who I was, or who I wanted to be?

Am I writing to be remembered?
Or am I writing to forget?
Are my words a disguise, or a truth surrendered?
I haven't found an answer to that yet.

I can't ignore the sadness that's hung
Where memories sit upon my wall,
Of when I was only good at being young,
And could still see the beauty of it all.

Do I just pretend I've forgotten?
The mind forgets but the heart does not,
Ruins of affairs, asking to be left unwritten,
Persist within my brain no matter what.

To forget the sermons from my youth,
That imprison me in a cage of my belief,
I search through wise men's writing for the truth,
Which only displaces my brittle hope with grief.

My life now runs on memories
In an age of untruths and illusion,
Filling my brain with half-remembered treacheries,
Blurring the lines between reality and delusion.

I used to tell lies worth believing,
Now when I write I am trying to be true,
But I find it is myself I am deceiving,
When the words I believe in aren't the words I choose.

Can I forget the wounds inflicted
By those bigots living in my head?
Can I forget the apologies that were rejected
By all those injured by the words I've said?

Is it too late to gain forgiveness
For any hurtful things I've done?
Is there anyone left who will bear witness?
Can guilty memories ever be outrun?

One day I too will be forgotten,
My final manuscript approved,
I hope to live on after I have fallen
Inside the memory of those that I have loved.

WRITING WAS NOT THE ANSWER
Being a poet means living with a permanent wound.

He started writing
Just to head off all the pain,
He started writing
It was all that kept him sane.

He aimed by writing
To imprison images in words,
Memories retaining
Using adjectives and verbs.

No other's writing
The soul's demand fulfilled,
He started writing
Before all good words were killed.

Now he was writing
Lines previously unheard,
Some solace finding
In the beauty of the word.

He kept on writing
Just to keep the hope alive,
It stopped him thinking
If he was going to survive.

He'd hoped the writing
Would replace the love that died,
But he tired of fighting,
Yearnings left unsatisfied.

He found his writing
Were truths told by a liar,
His words were dying
Like love without desire.

His love of writing
Killed by comments critics made,
Their words were biting
And cut him like a blade.

In the end the writing
Added darkness to distress,
Demons uniting
Until his own life mattered less.

The other writers
Let wreaths of words drop down
To float upon the water,
While they watched the poet drown.

THE SINGER
Fame and insecurity often prove a fatal combination.

She sang her songs, she made her mark,
But lived her life inside the dark,
No moon to shed its silvery light
To help her through the black and lonely night.
She was going down, was in freefall
To a river of treasons beyond recall,
Wanted to be who she was before,
A guilt-free, visionary troubadour.

Then Vodka's voice whispered in her ear
'You know that I can kill your fear,
Without the comfort that I bring
Could you ever write, would you ever sing?'
She knew well that voice's liquid charms
Surrendering into its arms,
It held her heart, she could write again,
A halfway happy with an edge of pain.

She wrote to lose herself in rhyme
There was a scar in every line,
Writing of a love she'd never see
Dreaming of the girl she used to be.
Escaping from the depths of her regret
The words she wrote were darker yet,
The hurt was all that she could sing,
To her, reality was an ugly thing.

She tried to escape the misery,
Taking back what she'd given free,
Skeletons of lovers killed by her art
Hung from the gallows of her heart.
She had become what she once hated,
Troubled by the person she'd created,
The Nightingale fell silent in the end,
Only she could be her own best friend.

Her life ran too close to the fire
Over broken glass and razor wire,
She reaped the pain that she had sown
Her tears left to dry out on their own.
Living in the solitude of fame,
Finding no one but herself to blame,
She sank to an ultimate defeat,
Back to Black on infinite repeat.

(*Memories of Amy Jade Winehouse 1983 - 2011*)

WATCHWORD
I had good reasons for learning to read, poetry wasn't one of them.

Words stare out at me from the screen's constraint
Daring me to hit that button marked delete,
They watch me accusingly, as if asking why
Lines should be killed before the poem is complete.

They don't realise this writer shares their pain,
Reluctant to consign words to the bin of history
That were paid for with anguish and precious time,
Torn so reluctantly from the memory.

I alter some words to satisfy my desire
For order, I have wounded them, they bleed,
Making me doubt those niggardly corrections.
It is as if they do not want me to succeed.

I have left the tracks of my life in my lines,
They have seen me from each and every side,
Each word is a fingerprint of my true self,
Some are objects of regret, others of pride.

Poems are the punctuation marks of my life,
Unexpected treasures and literary crimes.
My harshest critics are the words themselves,
Some are always with me, some are out of time.

These words that watch me malevolently now
Have already lived in some other writer's head.
They will outlive me, they were only borrowed,
I've never said anything not already said.

Do not think words are uncaring of their use
Cruel choices may have unintended consequence,
Think before you write, the words are watching,
Show them some love in your search for eloquence.

BEYOND THE BOUNDARY OF LANGUAGE
If you have nothing to say, better not to say it.

Silence is that grey area between yes and no
Which saves us from the mindless stupidity of words,
Can make even a fool appear to be wise,
And allow our whispered lies to be overheard.

Who has not felt the sharp stab of a lover's silence
Demanding you pause to look at who you really are,
Your love hidden within the chaos of your thoughts,
Lying in the lonely silence of words you cannot hear?

It would be better if words were only spoken when
Of more importance than any silence they replace.
Many absolute truths arise out of absolute silence,
It surrounds what's important with non-judgemental space.

In the silence far away from the fields of slaughter,
Where the sound of screams drown out the sacred hymn,
Are we who stay silent better than hypocrites who speak?
With our silence do we become an accomplice to their sin?

Silence may be used to reinforce good or evil intent,
To suppress opposition or as an aid to inspiration.
We should take as much care when using silence
As we would when using any other form of expression.

A pin-drop silence is to me the most precious thing,
It is free in the unlikely event that it can be found,
To find truth you have to become part of that silence,
Facing your true self normally guarded by sound.

I hide my voice behind those verses I never show,
My silence holding close the secrets of my poetry,
Hiding all of those words that wise men never speak
That would reveal a smouldering, unheard sophistry.

When below autumn skies, that are as smooth as glass,
I stand in the dawn light with heaven crying on my face,
And everything is transfixed so only the light moves,
Silence will come to hold me in its spiritual embrace.

In the dying arms of midnight just before sleep,
With eyelids closed I hold the silence up to my ear,
It is damp earth after rain, it's the colours of the wind,
The essence of a sound that is too beautiful to hear.

Silence goes beyond the boundaries of language,
Maybe the most insightful thought a poet can bequeath,
What we leave unsaid is our ultimate disguise
Up to that unanswerable silence of our last breath.

DISILLUSION
Adults aren't perfect, but children think they should be.

Children are the closest thing I've found to wisdom,
The young look at the world in a different way.
They believe they are able to write their own script,
Looking at a faster future that will fit a faster breed,
Not interested in what we did in our yesterday.

Caught in the confusion of an unintended world
The young lean on luck to avoid coming to harm,
Not grown up, but just learning to act like an adult,
Living in their own times, without our expectations,
Stealing from their mouths to feed their hungry arms.

They can't hear you and don't want what you have,
Their ship of dreams sitting out beyond the blue,
They are searching for a mirror that will tell them
Not who they really are but what they want to be,
Caught up in the storm of different points of view.

Children used to be taught the value of sacrifice,
Hard work was the price paid so you'd understand.
Now education is in danger of becoming
Synonymous with brainwashing of the young,
Now it's hip to be stupid and wear the right brand.

They will find lies do not constitute an argument,
That effort combined with indifference to failure
Is the real formula for success in any field,
Parents aren't perfect, teachers don't know it all,
Their words matched in no way by their behaviour.

They dream of building a better, kinder place,
Where love would make a difference to their lives,
But find that the only ticket that they can buy
Is for a one-way journey down towards disillusion.
When a child grows, that's when another dreamer dies.

Soon enough they will find their youth is getting old,
That there is no way to recover experiences missed,
They have just been skating on the surface of life
With all of the knowledge drifting underneath.
Few, if any, of their early dreams will persist.

In time they will find it is their past experiences
That are the essence of the intellect behind their name,
And all they really share is just this same existence,
With all of life's lessons learned a little too late,
And that this is life, it's just the nature of the game.

HEAT
Sunshine is our most precious gold.

We only get to see the sunrise
If we make it through the night,
Into the lukewarm of the morning,
And the sun's welcoming light.
All winter through we longed
To see that burnished golden sun,
Counting off the days to when
That summer warmth would come.

Then suddenly, when it comes
That heat begins to rise,
As the sun emerges from behind
Her winter cloud disguise.
But then the sun starts shining
And soon becomes our enemy,
We find we have no defense
Against such malevolent intensity.

The air is hanging heavy
Below the thirsty trees,
The atmosphere perfectly still
Without the comfort of a breeze.
The setting of the fireball
Gives us no relief at all,
The day's heat stored, then released,
From oven dried earth and red brick wall.

We pray for a reprieve
From the oppressive heat,
Shade was never so welcome,
Water never tasted quite so sweet.
A Mackeral sky is signalling
That there are cooler days to come,
But we know that fickle memory
Will soon long again for sun.

HOLDING ON TO LIFE

It takes a person who is in control of who they are to cast a non-judgmental eye over who they once were.

NO ONE'S KEEPING THE SCORE
If you feel a failure, let go, nobody cares as much as you think they do.

Fate sends us where we need to be,
In the end that's where we'll stand,
We are all running round in circles
Pretending that's what we planned.
Poets try vainly to say how this feels
With the meagre words at their command.

We all make our own history,
We'll never be who we want to be,
Or see all we want to see,
No one's interested in how it used to be.

It's easy to preach salvation when
Someone else's neck is on the line,
No one knows your vulnerability
Like enemies when a truce is signed.
Leaving never hurts as much
As does being left behind.

Who wants to leave is the one who will stay,
Nonbelievers are the ones who will pray,
He who has nothing is the one who will pay,
Whatever we want, all we have is today.

How will I pay when the
Stockpile of my debts comes due?
Where will I hide from the truth
When my fantasy is through?
Will I just drown like a sun
Bleeding into the blue?

I walk between disgust and temptation,
Avoiding a liar's humiliation,
Honesty lost in the translation,
Truth an individual calculation.

In the silence I can hear the blood
Whispering through my veins,
Silence strips everything from me
Until only the soul remains,
Any love I've been given torn apart
Just so that I can feel the pain.

Trapped within my own delusion,
Comforted by the warmth of love's illusion,
Protected by self-imposed seclusion
From life's continuous confusion.

I tried to put my life inside a sentence
Failing due to the inadequacy of words,
Becoming just another lost prophet,
Another face in the broken hearted herd,
Responsible for everything I wrote,
Every failure one I had deserved.

Life's a fleeting act of pantomime,
Guilt is a game for one by design,
I tried to bind my wounds with rhyme,
In the end we're all exposed by time.

The final poem lies there unfinished
The last words from a rheumatic hand,
My dreams buried in the rubble
Of the castles I left unmanned,
Verses that have been left unread
That only I could understand.

Abandoned poems lie like jetsam on the shore
I've forgotten the causes they were written for,
Although I wanted to win others wanted it more,
But it doesn't matter, no one's keeping the score.

LOOKING BACK
The afternoon knows what the morning never suspected.

I see my past divided into squares,
By loyal friends and disloyal lovers
By lines of elation and despair,
By triangular affairs with others,
By my own hypocrisy that time uncovers.

I see picture-perfect memories
Appear one by one framed by my door,
As seen through windows of a night-time train.
I can see things more clearly than before,
The failures too numerous to ignore.

I remember the over-optimism of youth,
And reminisce on the days of innocence,
Often mistaking consensus for the truth,
With inexperience my singular defense,
Only seeing my life in the present tense.

I envied men for their possessions
And for all their transient treasures,
I bought the fakes, sold what was real,
Bypassed love for instant pleasures
From easy women and hopeful wagers.

I stand here within my own silence
Like a man who is sure of what is true,
Surrounded by all those of no belief
With fake morality we all see through,
A hypocrite's masquerade of virtue.

I live now in the shadow of my yesterdays,
Soon will come the time for my goodbyes,
The halo of my few virtues fading away,
Leaving my life a square with equal sides,
Of joy and misery, honesty and lies.

Will I have that near death experience?
Will my past life scroll down before my eyes?
Will I just pass through into nothing,
Into that square where all energy dies?
Or will I be in for a surprise?

BEFORE INNOCENCE WAS LOST
I live with the loss of innocence and the inability to do it again.

The future is now so close,
Something I can almost see
Mixed up with paranoid delusions of reality.
I see the countless faces
Of those already come and gone
Still holding on to sterile dreams of better things to come.
All the familiar figures
Are fading to a silhouette,
I'm running along the mortal edge held back by my regret.
I have no cause left to fight for
Nothing for me to defend,
One step into the future, just a step nearer the end.

Give me back real rock and roll,
Wurlitzer juke box on the wall,
Eddie Cochran's Summertime Blues,
Buddy Holly and Peggy Sue,
Fats Domino on Blueberry Hill,
Riding my Triumph Bonneville.
Things judged by beauty not by cost,
Before our innocence was lost.

I'm running in circles down a
One way track of circumstance,
Questions that besiege me a testament to ignorance.
All the men of science with
The data that they gather,
Said they'd improve my life if they knew just what to measure.
Children look to me for guidance,
As I know they must,
Those who I myself would ask are already turned to dust.
As a last resort I pray
To open up the skies of mercy,
Now only death separates me from eternity.

Give me back hand written mail,
Pixie cuts and pony tails,
Mini-skirted girls who jive,
A time when drugs kept you alive.
Dad's Army, On The Buses,
Bridget Bardot and other crushes,
Before the PC lines were crossed
Before our innocence was lost.

The palaces now stand
Where coffins once were laid,
The horrors of belief disguised by hypocrisy's crusade.
Religious bleeding hearts,
That aim with their compassion
To soothe the broken heart, can't cancel out temptation.
Everyone knows someone
Needing something to believe in,
But if you have no god or faith where then is your sin?
Nothing's left of the beginning,
The end's close enough to see,
But I'll give you the future, the past's where I want to be.

Give me back respect for truth,
For the energy of my youth,
The sweetness of that first real kiss,
All the love that I now miss,
Belief in God's almighty plan
And faith in my fellow man,
Before my headstone is embossed,
Before my innocence is lost.

LOSING THE LIGHT

I am growing old, and my future is already behind me.

I am riding on a train of consequence
With no more stations on the line,
Everything is fading, I'm losing the light
I am being slowly buried by my life,
Following the darkness into the night.

In every direction that I look
I see strangers looking back at me,
With hearts uncovered and sarcastic eyes,
Just waiting for the whole world to turn
So that darkness will cover their lies.

I'm just a lonely whisper in the darkness
Original thoughts forgotten right away,
No longer knowing what words mean.
Now my lines are just idle repetition
And love's just another place I've been.

Some lines I write so that I feel good,
Some lines I write just for the hurt
With words never meant to rhyme.
Here in the shadow of life's promises
I am running out of words and time.

My poems are clothed in my loneliness
I punctuate them with my discontent,
Lines bleeding into black from blue,
Faded phrases leaving nothing behind
But disappearing traces of you.

Then when the night comes crawling in
And the silence grows too loud to hear,
My voice is lost in poems of death and love,
With remaining hopes for resurrection fading,
In the end you find even love is not enough.

The day grows as cold as a serpent's kiss,
Raindrops die against the heartless window,
Running down like the fears on my face.
There is nothing to be gained now
By any further explanation.

JUST ANOTHER POEM

I painted my self-portrait in 50 shades of blue and
in this moment of weakness I'm showing it to you.

Living alone in the emptiness of no man's land
I've been masquerading as someone who cares,
Wearing a poet's disguise and Trojan horse smile,
Clothes woven from lies and unanswered prayers.

A prism of pragmatism in a trial and error world,
Hiding here in the shadow of all my mistakes,
With secrets I'm not prepared to share or keep,
Held tight in the arms of eccentricity's embrace.

An outsider wanting to be back on the inside,
On the other side of love wearing tomorrow's smile.
I am playing my part so well that no one can tell,
It's too late to change, I'm too old to stand trial.

I travel with a suitcase full of empty dreams
With my memories all being eaten up by rust,
I leant on their promises but dreams came undone,
Falling through the cracks in the walls of my trust.

I'm waiting for an apology from the dream dealers
Who promised to build me an endless paradise,
But confession never comes easily to guilty men,
We only find the truth when it's too late to be wise.

I look into the mirror, it's not telling me any lies,
I see the reflection of a man I should have known,
I'm looking at the ghost of the man I used to be
With not even a medal for the courage that I've shown.

Just another poem that no one but you will ever hear
From a tired pen that's forgotten how it all began,
Shining a fading light into unknown, unowned spaces,
Illuminating only the quiet workings of a broken man.

EVALUATION
Could I have accomplished more if I'd been immune to boredom?

Am I satisfied with what I have achieved?
I never conquered any mountain's icy peak,
Or fought in a war where I defended freedom,
I failed my Latin and never attempted Greek.
It's true I used to be an athlete in my youth
But in all other sports was failed by my physique.

I travelled the world at someone else's expense,
But took my culture with me for safety's sake,
Made no attempt to learn a foreign language
To avoid embarrassment in case of a mistake.
My aversion to all things foreign just a defense
Against changes I wasn't prepared to make.

I acquired some level of professional status,
I suppose it could be said I tried to do my best,
But looking back on all of my achievements
I could not say I was any better than the rest.
I didn't always stand up for who or what was right,
Attempting to hide wrongs in which I acquiesced.

It is unlikely anyone will teach me anything that's new,
Or tell me the direction in which my life should turn,
But they may help me remember the things I always knew
And put me on the right path before I crash and burn,
Because I've found that often it's the easy lessons
That are the hardest ones for me to learn.

I look for an island of pride in my ocean of regret,
Have I built up more than I've torn down?
Did I write poetry that could affect another life,
Or was it written just because I liked its sound?
What is a poet anyway but a dissatisfied man,
Searching for a truth that cannot be found?

Having looked back at my life I cannot say
I am much wiser now than before I started.
The real questions are buried deep inside me,
Hidden from outsiders and closely guarded.
The answers are ones I alone can give,
To be revealed only after I've departed.

MEMORIES

When young I had aspirations that never came to pass,
now I'm old I have reminiscences of what never happened.

I am living inside my memories,
I'm just a visitor inside my brain,
A tenant in my body looking out of
The windows of my eyes. If I'm ever
Found out I'll be registered insane.

I've spent most of my time trying to write
Searching for a better word for love,
But know for every poem I've written
There's another I should have burned,
And what I write is never good enough.

I understand words that come too easy
Sometimes tell the bigger truth.
My best beginnings come from underneath the old,
And ghosts in my mind often discover
Half-remembered teachings from my youth.

I wake up each and every morning
Hoping to be relieved of yesterday's sin.
Overlapping memories still haunt me
Making me question what I knew, until now
It's not dying that scares me but the living.

I walked through scorn filled halls to see
A gypsy girl just to get my fortune read,
I wanted to know what my future held,
But then I put my fingers in my ears
So I couldn't hear what it was she said.

Why is there always pain inside of happy?
Why always lies hiding beneath the truth?
I tell myself I am still searching for
All of those things that money can't buy,
And for all the lost loves of my youth.

I didn't always get what I wanted
But at least I have learnt to pretend.
I can only tell you that everyone
Has got something, but no one has it all,
That's about all that I've learnt in the end.

TOUCHED BY POETRY
Poets are able to gaze into the darkness of their own hearts.

Everything our hands can reach out and touch
Is destined to degrade and to decay,
Only our dreams cannot be touched,
Poems are just dreams seen in another way.

Poetry can show you what cannot be seen,
When you are out of touch it lets you feel,
It can take you to where no one's ever been,
Things you didn't know you knew revealed.

Poetic words are moulded from our tears,
Carved from the stockpile of our pain,
Distilled from our love, our hopes and fears,
Mined from the dark caverns of the brain.

Poetry will take you out past the limit
Into Eden to taste forbidden fruit,
Its words make hidden thoughts explicit
Taking you closer to the absolute.

Poets assemble thoughts they've heard
Stealing any emotions they can find,
Then endeavour to set down in words
Truths you've kept hidden in your mind.

Poets dig their own literary trenches
In which they can be buried alive,
By all the lines they have discarded
To help a few of their poems survive.

Poetry can touch you in the places
That no human hand can ever go,
With its words, and even in its spaces,
It will touch your soul and you will know.

A poet can only offer up his rhyme
What it makes you feel is up to you,
A poet hopes to touch a life sometime
That life their only legacy that's true.

I started writing in the darkness,
I've tried to move back into the light,
But know I'll probably be remembered
Only for those poems I didn't write.

DREAMS AREN'T WHAT THEY USED TO BE
Memories beckon to me from the edge of my dreams.

Some days I want to go back
To when my mind was still intact,
To days when I was young enough to wonder.
Life was just a game we played
We still hadn't learned to act,
We had still yet to satisfy our hunger.

We were living undiscovered
Underneath a thin disguise
Of counterfeit, grown-up sophistication,
Confident in the knowledge
We knew that we were wise,
Happy we were the chosen generation.

They say we had it all
But that's not how it seemed,
We were full of smug, self-righteous anger.
We wrote songs to change the world,
At least that's what we dreamed,
But love died before we got to sing the encore.

Despite fate's disappointments
Some dreams are still intact,
Dreams take me out beyond the horizon line,
But dreams are not reality
I know that for a fact,
Fading from view as truth and life combine.

We thought we were on solid ground
Now we are drowning in the sea,
We've been fantasising rich while living poor,
Living for tomorrow
For things that couldn't be,
Reality lost inside our dreams of grandeur.

Now my dreams fly forward
Way above my past,
Old empty promises fill my veins with lies.
My future's already fixed
I know the die is cast,
All that remains in the end are goodbyes.

If only I could use
My dreams to neutralise
The carnage wrought by a million mistakes,
Now only the remnants
Of those not realised,
Lie buried deep within the ruins of my face.

I bought tickets with tears,
Said that's all I'd ever spend
On love, where results weren't guaranteed.
I wound up spending all I had,
Heart running on empty in the end.
Lennon was wrong, love isn't all you need.

The bird has flown
That hatched my dreams,
Leaving just memories burnt into my brain,
Full of lost chances
And might-have-beens,
Only the shadows of lost love remain.

I gave life everything
Even all my broken parts,
But still my life is not free of all regret.
Every dream I dreamed
Is written on my heart,
Few of them have been realised as yet.

I cry only because
I don't know what else to do,
Although no one is there to hear my tears fall,
The gods know what's coming
They have the perfect view,
My destiny is a future someone else will call.

Maybe my dreams will be
A reality tomorrow,
Once more I have put my misery on display,
You know me well by now,
Your student of sorrow,
Living far from paradise for yet another day.

RUNNING OUT OF TIME
I'd rather be told a cruel truth than live a comfortable delusion.

Do you get that feeling you are running out of time,
A long faded bloom among the flowers of the young?
Has the last glass of wine already been poured?
Is the party now all but over and the last song sung?

Are you one of those fully paid up losers of a sort
Traveling blindly down the path of nevermore,
Walking backwards over your own footprints
To answers you find that you've found before?

When lost in my innocence future sins were hidden,
And the air was soft and smelled of rain,
I was looking at the world with eyes wide shut,
Now I know no one's perfect and everyone's to blame.

Sitting behind walls holding the stories of my life,
I never could distinguish truth from false alarms,
I watched even the dearest of friends disappear,
Letting nostalgia hold me tightly in its arms.

In my garden of memories with heartache hedges,
I'm hoping I've left behind some reasons to be missed,
Apart from the ones who fell for each of my mistakes,
And all the would-be lovers whose lips were never kissed.
.

Today I will brave the cold graveyard rain alone
To place a single flower beneath that marbled name,
You find no pity in those silent ranks of stone,
Enemy or dearest friend, here they're all the same.

I drifted across life's seas until I ran aground
To where shadows of my past were all around,
Everyone here has their own sad story to tell
Ending up alone with their dreams worn down.

I never did find that place where words are born,
I searched every poetic line but haven't found it yet.
I look in the mirror to find the one who is to blame,
Seeing only the image of a poet lost in his regret.

All I am left with are some random bits of paper,
Filled with my unused and imperfect thoughts
Of half-remembered, awkward conversations,
Which sadly represents the sum of all I've got.

THE BEGINNING OF THE END
I seem to have been elbowed aside by a parody of myself.

I started out with nothing
And I've still got most of it left,
I got good grades, for what it's worth,
But not a shred of wisdom.
My poetry is all hard won,
Except that gained by theft,
I am a man of hindsight
Rather than one of vision.

Betrayed by advancing years
The words I am now writing
Only the ghosts of my old
Schoolmasters would speak.
There is nothing new in
The poems I am reciting,
My mistake was thinking
That I could be unique.

I've kept my real self a secret
From most of those I've known,
Good at making bad mistakes
But not owning them for long.
I regret all the time spent
Pretending, standing alone,
Rarely having the courage
To admit when I was wrong.

I made love part of my journey,
Or was it my destination?
Love's horizon deceives you
Often staying out of reach,
I tried to calculate a finality
But love got lost in the equation,
It escaped my feeble attempts
To capture it in speech.

It's too late now for me to write
Any memorable love songs,
I thought that a broken heart
Would write the perfect line,
But found that it was just
Something else I got wrong.
Another of life's betrayals,
Nostalgia camouflaged by time.

I have watched as all of my
Heroes have left before me,
A sign that I am approaching
The inescapable end.
All my good lines are still
In the garden of my memory,
But memory has no future,
I've run out of time to pretend.

WITCHES

Doubt is an uncomfortable condition that kills dreams.

Witches of doubt come from the hills
Riding the night winds,
They make love to the darkness
Laughing at my sins.

I thought I'd burned those witches
Forgetting what they said,
But nothing erased the disbelief
They left there in my head.

This doubter's belief is fragile
And easily undermined,
Sometimes all you want to do
Is walk out on your mind.

Are any of us deserving
Of the healing of the heart,
Where forgiveness and compassion
Both must play their part?

Have any of us the right to claim
Mercy for our soul,
While we hide in godless mansions
Paying homage to our gold?

Our dreams are being killed by the
Tears of our mistakes,
Our search for love is drowning in
A sea of rusting faith.

My tears only served to feed
The delirium machine,
My gods fell asleep and died within
The borders of my dream.

My backwash travelled with me
Rising up into my eyes,
Of all those I had sacrificed
In order to survive.

Many of my old certainties
Are proving to be untrue,
Leading me to question
Everything I knew.

I've become an artist of emotion
A master of deceit,
Appearing chameleon-like
To everyone I meet.

I suspect offers of divine rewards
Just flatter to deceive,
Wanting any promises in writing
Before I will believe.

I searched for truth without success
No matter how I tried,
Is it revealed to us only when
We're to be crucified?

I'm a not so beautiful ruin, built from
The splinters of my youth,
Knowing that often fear and lies are
More persuasive than the truth.

I see every day of life fate
Forces me to choose,
Between those things I want, and what
I'm prepared to lose.

Although my old holiness
Has faded from my view,
I hope that some old virtues
Are still just showing through.

IS DEATH WORTH LIVING FOR?
You think I know more than I do, because I'm older than
when you didn't think I knew as much as I did.

I am imprisoned by the walls of my own memories
Standing on the ashes of the bridges I have burned,
My knees buckling under the weight of the cross,
Wanting more from life than I have ever earned.

Living for a heaven that might not even be there,
Neither loving nor hating somewhere in between,
My world full of unknown things that are still to come,
The wind whispering rumours of what might have been.

I love all of the pleasure and curse the pain,
Searching for a light in the deep shadows of doubt,
With only love to fill up the cracks in my soul,
Knowing life is a dead end and there is no way out.

I'm just beginning to know what I used to believe,
Walking that narrow line between truth and lies,
Using words as weapons and silence as my shield
In that little world of blame where all loyalty dies.

I am making more promises I know I cannot keep,
Eating the darkness, bringing emptiness crashing in,
No longer making a shadow when I walk in the sun,
Wondering if I have room to hide just one more sin.

I fashioned lies from the images of angelic faces,
Kept the war going just so that I could feel the pain,
Aware of everything and yet aware of nothing at all,
Dredging up scraps of buried souls just to love them again.

Only if they look into my eyes will they see the scars,
Cold fingers trace my wounds by the graveyard's light,
A road map of all the pointless battles I have fought,
Blood shed in vain struggling to do what was right.

My dreams have all been buried deep in the rubble,
All I wanted was to be on the other side of misery,
Knowing I'd never escape from what I'd become
After I realised suicide is not a matter of degree.

I never claimed to have the answers but faked it pretty well,
Still seeking salvation when there was nothing left to save,
Wrote poems made of whispers, a silent chorus of the dead,
Not realising I was already dancing on my own grave.

I've lived in someone else's dream but will die in my own,
Now I only want all those things that money can't buy,
If I found a death worth living for it wouldn't take me alive.
If only I could find someone who'd tell me what it's like to die!

ADDRESS BOOK
I count my age by friends, not by possessions or accomplishments.

Names that used to lead me
To the phone hung on the wall,
Now stare out accusingly,
Victims of my procrastination,
Of unwanted conversations.

Standing in the rush of time
The names unfold before me,
They define my reality,
Forgotten appointments,
Delights and disappointments.

Flat lines bisecting so many,
Are horizontal markers of death,
Reflecting lost heartbeats.
The few without corrections
Ever more precious in my affections.

The pages hold too many truths,
Times of celebration
And of reckoning,
A requiem recorder,
But I'm comforted by its order.

I retain it despite deletions,
The remaining names useful
Only to inform others
When I've finally gone away.
It smells of yesterday.

THE PIPER HAS TO BE PAID
In life there are no free lunches.

With age I saw my dreams of optimism recede
Finding truth quite different than what I once believed,
The bitter disappointment of maturity persists
For which, as yet, I've found no remedy exists.
I left some early dreams behind for others to retrieve.

I tried to hold the line, I tried to stand against the tide,
But my grip on what I used to know soon began to slide,
Yes I felt the flame of revolt and revolution
And offered up a young man's simplistic solution,
But age opens up the heart to show the lies inside.

Those early years of hope and expectation,
With heroes there to provide my inspiration,
Could not survive reality's harsh light
And, as sure as the day is eaten by the night,
My achievements fell well short of expectations.

Of all my dreams that came and disappeared
It was only love that survived across the years,
Not forever though, as we are mortal creatures,
Love left, with Cohen crying through the speakers,
And I was left with only heartbreak souvenirs.

The accumulated guilty verdicts must be obeyed
It's too late for reparations to be made,
I'd ask for mercy if I could only find my voice,
Judgements are harsh, it is now Hobson's choice,
I know the Piper always has to be paid.

AN HONEST MAN
The only honest things we do are done when we're alone.

The rain falls down on the honest man
Slowing the blood running in his veins,
His life a stone that's thrown and sinks
Until not even a ripple remains,
While his history is just a recipe
For every earthly pain.
The cold rain of oblivion
Falls down on the honest man.

He conspires like any other man
To make his life mercifully brief,
It's all too much, but not enough
To rationalise his belief.
His honesty is what hurts him,
Only the lies bring some relief,
Futile prayers from Bible or Koran,
Fall down on the honest man.

Although his life was like everyman
It had never been lived before,
He feels guilty for his innocence
And for what he's hoping for.
He damns the dream that steals his night,
The one that robs his soul hurts more.
Tears for a life that hasn't gone to plan,
Fall down on the honest man.

Neither libertarian nor Presbyterian
His history is drowning in mystique,
He can't distinguish truth from anger,
Or the commonplace from unique.
He feels he's diving into irrelevance
Among the worthless words we speak,
Sins of the saints and barbarian
Fall down on the honest man.

To him love's just a declaration of compromise
That is spilt from a liar's tongue.
The honest man has learnt to turn and face
All the things he can't outrun,
Knows the life he's lived is the one he'll lose,
He'll mourn what he has done.
The blood of the communion
Falls down on the honest man.

He is deeply drowning, reaching for dry land,
Hoping his faith will be enough,
Trying to live his life as if this moment
Is the last chance he has to love.
Making his own way through life's illusion
Hoping for guidance from above,
Drops of mercy leaking through God's hand
Fall down on the honest man.

A bit of everyone since his life began
Has soaked into his skin,
He has realised that so-called reality
Only truly exists within,
He's asking now, before the end,
How did it all begin?
The same rain that fell on Adam
Falls down on the honest man?

The rain falls down on the honest man
And on every liar's grave,
Rain stains the marble a darker black
Reflecting those he has betrayed.
You can see the rain inside his eyes
For a life he has outstayed,
That heartless rain of life's finite span
Falls down on the honest man.

SOUL
Our soul contains the memory of our true nature.

I have mislaid my soul somewhere
Between the sermon and the gold,
I've only just become aware
Now my body's growing old.
I'm hanging onto the edge of life
So close to falling off,
Thinking nobody would blame me
If I said I'd had enough.

I'm here with all the treachery
I thought I'd left behind,
Trying to set my soul free,
Trying to turn back time.

I am sounding out the silence
Avoiding all the words,
They're no more than a contrivance
Of things I may have heard.
If I look hard I can see the cracks
Of doubt are running through,
All the truths that I was taught,
All the words I thought I knew.

I wonder who will speak for me
When the bells of heaven chime,
Trying to set my soul free,
Trying to turn back time.

I'm a little further from perfection
With every year gone past,
Swimming towards perception
But the current is too fast.
I must have paid for my success
With all of my defeats,
Every one of my advances
Being matched by my retreats.

It is the hidden cross I carry
That's put scars upon my rhyme,
Trying to set my soul free,
Trying to turn back time.

I've broken many promises
That I might yet regret,
Ignored many cries for help
That others won't forget.
Sometimes it might be better
If I just threw away,
The baggage I've been carrying,
And all I've learnt up to today.

Maybe I will never see
What it is that's truly mine,
Trying to set my soul free,
Trying to turn back time.

Lines written prove just a litany
Of loveless prose again,
Words that filled me up so quickly
But then are slow to drain.
What would I be sounding like
Without the words I'm wearing?
What would there be left of me
If I stopped pretending?

I'm sliding into irrelevancy
Within an orphaned mind,
Trying to set my soul free,
Trying to turn back time.

THE ENGLISHMAN
The Englishman admires the man who has no talent but is modest about it.

How sad he looks, this Englishman,
The hand of time having only gently
Blurred the features of his face.
Just another one of Darwin's children,
Evolved within times of plenty
Comfortable in his social place.

There is a line etched across his palm
Where his boundaries are drawn,
And where his history is displayed.
He has always tried to play the game,
Not as king or bishop more as a pawn,
But feels his debts have all been paid.

Many times he has had to walk behind
Other people's restless ambition,
His loyalty often tested by his regret.
He just needs friends, nothing more,
Accepting all of life's imperfections,
Knowing what you pay for is what you get.

He suspects his life has been lived before,
That all his words have been already said,
But he owns his verses and the odd bad rhyme.
His mind is as empty now as it has ever been,
But, when young, those things put in his head
Have all stayed there throughout his time.

He knows love that you give comes at a cost,
Now he can only afford love that's freely given.
He asks, what's the point of love you only borrow,
Which tiptoes down the backstairs of your life
When passion and desire are in remission,
Leaving you with nothing but lasting sorrow?

He hopes some memory of him will remain,
Not of one who was perfect just one who was kind,
Afraid he's now one of the people he struggles to praise.
His conscience, like the soft ache of a phantom limb,
Eats away contentment leaving only guilt in the mind,
Heightened by the Englishman's quixotic ways.

Maybe though the Englishman is not so sad
Having found that even sadness has its uses.
His dreams have slipped away by slow degree,
Yet he knows time is a battle nobody wins,
And life is not interested in his excuses,
But inside his heart the Englishman is free.

TOWARDS TRUTH
It's impossible to write the truth if you know someone else will read it.

These lines are for all those unread poems
I will leave behind,
Moments as yet unshared,
Favourite phrases not yet assigned.
Fragments of years once lived,
A masterpiece not yet begun,
Lines yet to soak up my tears
And the sadness from the sun.

I've been busy writing of futilities
Like most poets do,
Every word an understatement,
Every exaggeration true.
I searched for some certainty
By mining my empire of lies,
But what I thought was absolute
Were my own words in disguise.

In the pitch dark of a starless night
I try hard to forget
All the places almost visited,
All the people I almost met.
I add up all the zeros
In my book of might-have-been,
Its covers hiding my secret life
On the pages in-between.

In the deepest parts of my heart
I found the darkest art,
Secret thoughts kept undercover
From the very start.
They became my enemies,
My self and soul unmasked,
Giving me answers to the questions
I never should have asked.

I lack undeniable evidence
For creation or infinity,
No faith fills the space between
My gods and prophecy.
Without my lover's kiss
Even the sweetest things taste bitter,
I only have poetry's stitches now
To hold it all together.

Although I tried to learn
From everything I ever read,
Nothing I've written was as clever
As it sounded in my head.
I regurgitated words from
Some long-gone teacher's mouth,
All the allegories and myths
Told to me in lieu of truth.

I no longer get inspiration,
That will help me make my mark,
From legends of the past
Whispering to me in the dark.
At the margin of my dreams
Bright sparks of truth are forming,
Which turn black as my mood
Against the white lies of the morning.

I am making my own history
Living one day at a time,
The future is getting ever faster
Too far off now to be mine.
I hope to outlive my memories
And all the fears that live within,
And one day hope to be wiser
Than the total of my sin.

I travelled beyond the empty ruins
Of my ancestry,
Far past the pages of my belief
In any famous victory.
I tried spelling out the name of love
One letter at a time,
Having nothing left to offer
But inconsequential rhyme.

Sharp shards of broken promises
Litter the empty street
Where I walk towards finality
Upon my bleeding feet.
Clothed in a mournful melancholy
I carry my own wreath,
Feigned acceptance of the end
Covering cowardice beneath.

The marble slab is waiting
To be engraved, so passers-by
Remember the foolish heroes
It will cover when they die.
But I will not seek out danger,
I do not want it to be over,
I will leave the dead behind,
Take my chance and run for cover.

When you slip into the realm of hurt
Where there is only pain,
And the night comes in to claim
Any light that might remain,
You will be in that place
Where youth and laughter never go,
That I have already visited,
One you will get to know.

I cannot change reality it's locked up
In the words I breathe,
Or rearrange the letters
To find the beauty underneath.
I can't disguise in my eyes
A look that speaks of my regret,
Or hide my disappointment
That I haven't found truth yet.

I know mediocrity's rewarded
So I set my standards low,
While I haven't found the truth
Maybe it's better not to know.
Although within the words I've written
Hide every literary sin,
They show that behind the smile
There's a sadder soul within.

I watch my own deadline approach
Through a poet's eyes,
Wondering if that's when I'll get to see
Where forever dies.
I didn't mean to write darkly
But am guided by distrust,
I am like a fine rain that turns
Every shiny thing to rust.

I look out at the brave new world
Through old and jaundiced eyes,
If my melancholic musings
Have depressed you, I apologise,
But as you move into old age
From over optimistic youth,
You may find that my
Darkest verses are closest to the truth.

AM I WHAT I ALWAYS WANTED TO BE?
  Trying to find yourself is never easy.

I have yet to find any real solution
To my own inadequate evolution,
Having spent my life in fruitless searches
In countless bars and soulless churches,
Before finding my realities were an illusion.

A victim of capricious circumstance,
Humbled by my own ignorance,
With many parts of life still unplayed.
I made mistakes I wouldn't have made
If I could have lived life in advance.

I lack the wisdom or the imagination
To express the pain of love's final separation,
Waiting every hour just for the night to fall
As I tried but failed to make sense of it all.
Time did not heal or lead to revelation.

I'm no longer sure what time is meant to be
Whether it is my friend or my enemy,
Words like water falling farther from the rain,
Like embers burning farther from the flame,
Disappear into anonymous poetry.

I spew timeworn words I can't forget
Onto pages of resentment and regret,
Trying to resolve ill-defined questions
Unanswered still with other misconceptions,
But it's not over, I'm not finished yet.

There is much still left to discover
Before I break off and run for cover,
Many cerebral lines still to be written
Many unbelievers still to enlighten,
Before I'm prepared to say it's over.

I am still unsure yet if I've found me,
But senility, or a newfound humility,
May eventually give me the answer,
And in myself I'll see that hidden writer,
Finding I am what I always wanted to be.

STILL HOLDING ON
In the end nothing you can buy replaces any love you've lost.

Learning to live with myself took more than a lifetime,
Bitter the taste of truths I could not bear to face,
As was the sharp stab of pain felt in my heart
Of a lost love I could not replace.
Realising now that life's not a rehearsal,
Learning to live with the guilt of the past,
Standing safe inside your circle,
Approaching that final hurdle,
Holding on to any love I know will last.

Autumn leaves remind me another summer's come and gone,
But nature's colours have never changed.
For a hundred years the old masters in the gallery
Have always been perfectly arranged.
Only my life descends into disorder,
My heart in a race with my conscience,
Finding life gives no quarter,
As time gets ever shorter,
Holding on to love as my only defense.

You did not know that I was smiling secretly
Behind my poetic paper frown,
Making multihued mosaics out of our memories
To hold my innate sad feelings down.
I cannot provide redress to you accusers
For things I've said but can't retract,
But most were said with humour,
And I walk into the future
Holding on to my righteousness intact.

I have learned that life will pay you back
For every mistake you've ever made,
I'm happy, as I know any sanity lost,
Was worth the price that I have paid.
You have put the smile back on my face
Where all of the frown lines used to live,
The world's a less empty space,
My life is in a better place,
Holding on to the love you give.

I keep you in a safe place in my garden of poems,
You lifted me and convinced me to restart,
Helping me to see the world with an old man's brain
But still with a young man's heart.
Although I have that Bentley I couldn't resist,
A monument of sorts behind my garage door,
A Patek Philippe on my wrist
And other things from my list,
Holding on to you I value more.

I thought of leaving you some sort of explanation
Maybe a letter with the truth enclosed,
Detailing all the transgressions of my enemies
In which all of their lies would be exposed.
But you've read the words already written,
And all the emotions that they impart,
What I did that was forbidden,
All my sins that were forgiven,
Holding on to secrets still in my heart.

You've been the elusive spark of inspiration
That's behind every single line I write,
A revealing flash of incandescence
That comes shape-shifting in the night.
A poet would have found better words
But these were the best that I could do,
Monolithic truths I heard,
Both eloquent and absurd,
Holding on to the honesty of you.

I have tried hard to find an original line
Between what's art and what's plagiarised,
To take this last chance to tell you of love
That up to now I've kept well disguised.
My hesitancy you may well condemn,
My mind was way out in front of my heart,
Wrote letters, didn't send them,
Didn't know how to end them,
Holding on to you right from the start.

Only those of you who have been close to me,
Will even care or attempt to understand,
Why I've tried to write these words of explanation
And am leaving them safely in your hand.
Although scant reward for what you've given me,
This last poem has been written just for you,
Because in all reality
This poet that you see,
Has survived by holding on to you.

(*Those of you that matter know who you are.*)

153

*"There comes a time in
your life when you have
to choose to turn the page,
write another book
or simply close it."*

Shannon L. Alder

.

www.ingramcontent.com/pod-product-compliance
Lightning Source LLC
Chambersburg PA
CBHW070930130626
46555CB00001B/367